THE CURIOUS SAVAGE

BY JOHN PATRICK

DPS

DRAMATISTS PLAY SERVICE

"And if I laugh at any mortal thing—
'Tis that I may not weep."

—Byron

FOREWORD

A play comes to life only when the reader or actor is in sympathy with the playwright's intentions. The wrong interpretation of a play distorts its meaning. Overemphasis where none was intended destroys the delicate balance of values and the play then becomes either pointless or in bad taste.

It is important in "The Curious Savage" that the gentle inmates of "The Cloisters" be played with warmth and dignity. Their "Home" is not an "asylum" nor are these good people "lunatics." Any exaggeration of the roles will rob them of charm and humor. The whole point of the play is to contrast them with Mrs. Savage's children and the insane outside world. To depart from this point of view for the sake of easy laughs will rob the play of meaning. And both the performers and the playwright will have failed in their purpose.

JOHN PATRICK

THE CURIOUS SAVAGE was first produced in New York by The Theatre Guild and Lewis & Young, under the direction of Peter Glenville, at the Martin Beck Theatre, October 24, 1950, with the following cast:

The Guests:

FLORENCE	Isobel Elsom
HANNIBAL	Robert Emhardt
FAIRY MAY	Lois Hall
JEFFREY	Hugh Reilly
MRS. PADDY	Gladys Henson

The Family:

ETHEL SAVAGE	Lillian Gish
TITUS	Brandon Peters
SAMUEL	Howard Wendell
LILY BELLE	Marta Linden

The Staff:

MISS WILHELMINA	Flora Campbell
DR. EMMETT	Sydney Smith

Setting by GEORGE JENKINS

ACT I
SCENE 1. Night.
SCENE 2. The next morning.

ACT II
SCENE 1. That night, after dinner.
SCENE 2. A few nights later.

ACT III
A few minutes later.

The scene is the living room of "The Cloisters."

THE CURIOUS SAVAGE

ACT I

SCENE 1

The living room of The Cloisters in a town in Massachusetts. The room is large and charmingly furnished, with many deep chairs, covered in flounced chintz. The wallpaper is bright and in good taste. A large square rug covers most of the floor. There is a double sliding-door leading from the hallway stage R. *A single door, stage* L., *leads off to the front offices.*

AT RISE: *Fairy May stands gazing pensively out of the window upstage* C., *which overlooks the garden. Wan and slender, she is in her early twenties. Her dark hair emphasizes the pallor of her skin, a contradiction to her gay and sanguine nature. Hers is a classic beauty vitiated by the severe arrangement of her hair, an unimaginative dress, and steel-rimmed glasses. Jeffrey stands with his back to the audience, studying the book titles on the ceiling-high shelves. He is a handsome young man of about twenty-five, with the dignity of a much older man. Florence sits at a table downstage* C., *playing a game of Parcheesi with herself. She is about twenty-eight, gentle, eager to please, and somewhat inclined to be "elegant." A sweet and tremulous smile is her best and most disarming weapon. Hannibal belies his thirty years. He is pink, plump, and cherubic. He stands near the piano* R., *tuning his violin.*

FLORENCE. Is their car still in front, Fairy? *(When Fairy fails to answer, she looks up from her game.)* I said, is their car in front?
HANNIBAL. Oh, Fairy! *(Fairy starts, and turns to him.)* Florence

was speaking to you.

FAIRY. I'm sorry, Florence. I was watching the fireflies. What did you say?

FLORENCE. I said, can you see if they've left yet?

FAIRY. *(Shakes her head.)* I wish I'd been born a cat so I could see in the dark.

JEFF. I don't think I'll wait for her. I'm going to get a book and go to my room. *(He crosses down to Florence.)*

FLORENCE. *(Solicitously.)* Does your jaw hurt tonight, Jeff?

JEFF. Not bad.

FLORENCE. Then stay a little longer. We'd like to have you. *(She extends her hand fondly, which Jeff holds for a moment.)*

HANNIBAL. Jeff—you've already invested two hundred and sixty-seven minutes in waiting—surely you can afford an additional ten cents' worth.

JEFF. *(Smiles.)* All right, my statistical friend. My curiosity is good for ten minutes more. *(He goes back to the books as Fairy crosses down from window.)*

FAIRY. I wonder what she is like? Miss Willie says they are one of the wealthiest families in America.

HANNIBAL. *(Tuning his violin.)* Oh, that's bad. She'll have an expensive camera she can't work. *(Plunk.)* Or rave about an artist I never heard of. *(Plunk.)*

FAIRY. Oh—cynic! Has money spoiled *me*?

HANNIBAL. Do you have money, Fairy?

FAIRY. Bags.

FLORENCE. Let's not be prejudiced about money. Some of my best friends are wealthy. Hannibal—play something while we're waiting. Help distract Jeff.

HANNIBAL. Well—you catch me tuned. What shall it be? *(He comes down c.)*

FLORENCE. Surprise us.

HANNIBAL. How about a gypsy czardas? *(Puts violin under his chin.)*

FAIRY. Please don't play gypsy music, Hannibal. It frightens me.

HANNIBAL. *(Lowers violin.)* Frightens you?

FAIRY. Terrifies me. I was stolen by gypsies when I was a child and rescued just as they were about to dye my skin with walnut juice. *(When the others give her a reproving look, she protests.)* Well, I *was.*

FLORENCE. Go ahead, Hannibal. *(Hannibal again places violin under his chin—takes a stance—and pauses as Fairy looks toward door and interrupts.)*

FAIRY. I hope she likes music. Maybe she plays some instrument herself. The harp! Oh—I hope she plays a harp. All my life— *(She catches Hannibal's reproachful glance.)* I'm sorry, Hannibal. Go ahead. *(Sits down and folds her hands in her lap. Then sotto voce to Florence.)* I was *raised* on a harp. My father— *(Extends her hands harpist-fashion.)* Like an *angel!* *(Again Hannibal chins violin and stands poised. Folds the pose for a moment, then lowers instrument slowly. Jeff, at the bookcase up L., is taking short jumps into the air unaware of the imminent concert behind him.)*

FLORENCE. Jeff—what *are* you doing?

JEFF. Oh. There's a book I want on the shelf. I'm sorry, Hannibal.

FLORENCE. Fairy—get the book for Jeff so we can listen to Hannibal.

FAIRY. Wait, I'll get a chair. *(Brings chair up to the shelves.)*

JEFF. Never mind, Fairy, I can get it.

FAIRY. No, Jeffrey, climbing on chairs is women's work. *Men* have mountains. *(She stands up on chair.)* Which book did you want?

JEFF. *The Life Span of the Ape.*

FLORENCE. *(Rises and crosses to Fairy.)* People give the strangest books to this library. I couldn't get into *Forbidden Tibet.*

FAIRY. *(Turning to others.)* It's amazing what standing above people does. Do you know, I feel smarter than anybody in the whole world.

JEFF. *(Points.)* It's the yellow one.

FAIRY. Books are in my blood. My mother invented the filing system at the New York Library. She was "Queen of Cross-Index."

HANNIBAL. *(Puts down violin and crosses to Fairy.)* I'll get Jeff's book, Fairy.

FAIRY. No, no, no, no. Musicians shouldn't work. *(Turns to the books again.)*

FLORENCE. Be careful, Fairy—don't get dust in your eyes.

FAIRY. *(Reaches vainly, then turns back to Jeff.)* Wouldn't you like *Animal Husbandry*? I can reach that.

JEFF. This time it's got to be *The Life Span of the Ape.*

HANNIBAL. *(Hands violin bow to Fairy.)* Goose it out with this. *(In the midst of concentrated activity beside the bookcase, Mrs. Paddy enters and stands at doorway* R. *She is a dumpy, middle-aged woman of awesome ferocity. Her close-cropped hair bristles from her head with aggressive hostility. She is wearing a paint-smeared smock. She takes in the scene unobserved. She reaches for light switch and plunges the room into darkness. Hannibal shouts.)* Lights! Turn the lights back on!

FAIRY. Don't let me fall!

HANNIBAL. Please turn the lights back on.

FLORENCE. Hannibal, get to the switch before someone is hurt.

JEFF. *(Pause.)* It looks like Mrs. Paddy is back. *(Lights suddenly go on again. Facing Mrs. Paddy at light switch is Miss Wilhelmina. "Miss Willie" is an efficient and attractive girl of about twenty-four. She wears a tailored gray-blue suit with a flower in her lapel. Mrs. Paddy eyes her resentfully. The picture is held for a moment, and then Mrs. Paddy reaches out quickly and plunges the room into darkness again.)*

HANNIBAL. Lights! Lights! Lights!

FLORENCE. Please, Mrs. Paddy, let us keep the lights on. *(Miss Willie promptly turns lights on and protects switch with her palm. She reaches out with her other hand and, taking Mrs. Paddy's elbow, propels her toward window seat* C., *where an easel stands with the front of the canvas facing upstage. Mrs. Paddy sits down out of sight behind it.)*

MISS WILLIE. Some night you're going to turn out the lights at the wrong time and hurt somebody. Then you'll be sorry. I do wish you'd chosen something else to give up for Lent.

JEFF. It's unfair to make the rest of us suffer to get you to heaven, Mrs. Paddy.

FAIRY. Other people *like* electricity.

MISS WILLIE. Now you sit at your easel like a good girl. And leave the lights alone.

FAIRY. I must say you startled us, Miss Willie. We thought you were in the front office.

MISS WILLIE. *(Turns to look at Fairy, who stands on chair with bow in her hand.)* For the love of Pete, Fairy, what are you up to?

FAIRY. I was just trying to get a book for Jeffrey.

MISS WILLIE. With a violin bow?

FAIRY. I couldn't quite reach it.

JEFF. I certainly didn't mean to cause all this commotion. Forget it.

FAIRY. No—no—no. I'll get it for you. *(She turns back to shelf.)* Everyone watch his own head. Timber! *(Pulls book out of the case with bow, and it falls to the floor.)* There you are, Jeffrey. *(To Miss Willie.)* You may take the bow, Miss Willie. *(To Hannibal.)* You may take my hand, Hannibal. *(She steps down from chair.)*

MISS WILLIE. The next time anyone wants a book from the top, Fairy, call me. Why, the whole shelf might have fallen on you. *(Crosses R. to replace chair at desk.)*

FAIRY. *(Following.)* Oh, who ever heard of anyone being hurt by good books?

MISS WILLIE. Enough of them might, darling. And I'd hate that to happen.

MRS. PADDY. *(Rises from behind easel and announces to no one in particular.)* I hate everything in the world, but most of all I hate cold cream, hot dogs, codfish, crawfish, catfish, catnip, sheepdip, sawdust, subways, sewers, skewers, buttermilk, caterpillars, frictions, fractions, pins, puns, pens, policemen and electricity. *(The others pay no attention to Mrs. Paddy's recital and continue as if she had made no statement. She sits down again.)*

FAIRY. Miss Willie, how much longer do we have to wait?

FLORENCE. What is she like, Miss Willie?

MISS WILLIE. I haven't seen her. Let's tidy the room a bit. *(Stops at sofa and hands bow to Hannibal.)* Fairy, will you put the Parcheesi board away, please?

FLORENCE. They're taking an awfully long time in the front office.

FAIRY. Is she young or old, Miss Willie?

MISS WILLIE. *(Straightening the room.)* All I know is that her name is Savage—and she gets the Blue Room.

FAIRY. I hope she isn't beautiful. Competition exhausts me. *(She picks up small table with the Parcheesi board and carries it upstage.)*

MISS WILLIE. *(Stops in front of Jeff and adjusts his tie.)* Well, Bingo, you tied that one in a hurry.

JEFF. *(Patiently.)* Miss Willie, don't call me that—please. It's a pet name my wife uses.

MISS WILLIE. I forgot. *(Leans over and kisses him on the forehead.)*

JEFF. And I wish you wouldn't single me out to kiss.

MISS WILLIE. You're the handsomest.

JEFF. What would my wife think if she came to call and saw a strange woman kissing me? She'd explode.

MISS WILLIE. She would if I know her.

JEFF. Will you please try to remember?

MISS WILLIE. I'll try. Forgive me. *(House phone on desk rings. Miss Willie sighs, and crosses toward it.)*

FAIRY. Ting-a-ling-a-ling-a-ling. *(Picks up receiver and holds it out for Miss Willie.)*

MISS WILLIE. *(Takes phone.)* Hello. Yes, Doctor Emmett. Right away. *(She hands receiver back to Fairy.)* Put the dart board up, Hannibal. Please don't clutter the place, darlings. Let's make a good *first* impression. *(Starts out.)*

FAIRY. Will we meet her now?

MISS WILLIE. I don't know. *(Takes a key from her dress pocket, unlocks door L. and goes out, closing it behind her with a click. Fairy follows to door and stands looking at it.)*

FAIRY. We haven't had anyone exciting here since that magician's wife. Remember—she was all nerves from being sawed in half so much. What *was* her name?

HANNIBAL. *(Hanging dart board on U.S. wall.)* Something hyphenated.

FAIRY. I forget. But she had color. My relations are all so drab. Both my parents were albinos.

FLORENCE. Really, Fairy—you shouldn't invent such things!

FAIRY. Well, they were! *Emotional albinos. (Gets down on her knees to peer through keyhole.)*

FLORENCE. Oh, Fairy—don't peek. It's so degrading to get on your knees.

FAIRY. You get on your knees to pray, don't you? I'll say a prayer. Dear God—let me see something.

HANNIBAL. See anything?

FAIRY. Yes—I do. God was quick.

HANNIBAL. What do you see?

FAIRY. Someone coming out of Doctor Emmett's office.

FLORENCE. *(Rising.)* Who?

FAIRY. *(Counts.)* One—two—three strange people. *(Rises quickly.)* They're coming in here! *(Looks around excitedly.)* Let's hide in the hall and eavesdrop.

HANNIBAL. Is that ethical, Jeff?

FAIRY. You know we'll be sent out anyhow.

JEFF. We could call it espionage.

FAIRY. *(Quickly takes Mrs. Paddy by the hand and leads her to door* R.*)* Come, Mrs. Paddy—we're going to spy.

JEFF. I'll guard the light switch—it's rude to let guests enter a dark room.

FLORENCE. *(Following Fairy.)* This is the last time I'm going to be a party to peeking, Fairy. Kneeling simply ruins my nylons.

FAIRY. I mustn't get excited or I'll get hiccups and betray us. *(They disappear into hallway* R. *and close sliding doors behind them just before Miss Willie unlocks door* L. *She stands aside to admit Senator Titus Savage. Titus looks like a well-dressed businessman of conservative tastes. He is sober, humorless and direct. He is followed by his sister, Lily Belle. Lily Belle is tall, slender, chic and assured. The only situation to which she is unequal is her fortieth birthday. She is followed by her brother Judge Samuel Savage. Samuel is short, undistinguished, and somewhat lost in the penumbra of his brother's cold authority and his sister's brittle self-assurance.)*

MISS WILLIE. Doctor Emmett will join you in a moment.

TITUS. Please tell him that if there is nothing more—we'd like to get started back.

MISS WILLIE. Yes, Senator Savage. There are cigarettes and magazines on the table. Please make yourselves at home. *(Goes out.)*

LILY BELLE. *(Crosses down to sofa.)* Well, what do you think of it now, Titus? Are you reassured?

TITUS. Somewhat. It certainly doesn't look like an institution.

SAMUEL. Not at all.

LILY BELLE. Mother will be contented and happy here—I'm sure. It's a charming place.

TITUS. I just hope we haven't made a mistake.

LILY BELLE. Darling—the only mistake we made was in not taking steps sooner.

TITUS. I don't like to be thought insensitive. It might have been wiser to have kept her at home with an attendant.

LILY BELLE. That would have been disastrous.

SAMUEL. You're hard.

LILY BELLE. Someone has to be practical.

SAMUEL. No—you're calloused—you've married too many foreigners.

LILY BELLE. Samuel—darling—we've done what had to be done—let's not quarrel about it, please.

TITUS. Lily Belle is right. This is civilized behavior. *(Dr. Emmett enters L.)*

DR. EMMETT. I'm sorry to have delayed you. I was anxious to have Doctor Johnson question your mother.

TITUS. This is quite a place you have here, Doctor. It's been a great relief to us to have found it so cheerful.

LILY BELLE. But then, we were assured that your place offered the best that money could buy.

DR. EMMETT. We hope we offer the best that experience can provide.

TITUS. One thing I meant to ask you, Doctor—will Mother be exposed to any danger here?

DR. EMMETT. Not at all—the guests in this wing are in their final stage of treatment. They are extremely kind and cooperative. On the surface, most of them would seem quite as normal as, say, yourself, Senator.

TITUS. You don't say.

DR. EMMETT. While we're waiting, Senator—I'd like to ask a few more questions about this Memorial Fund of your mother's.

TITUS. There's little more to tell. She planned on using it to give away the entire Savage estate.

SAMUEL. The newspapers called it her Happiness Fund.

DR. EMMETT. Was this indifference to money something recent?

TITUS. I wouldn't say so.

LILY BELLE. She's always given money to foolish causes.

DR. EMMETT. Would you mind being more specific?

TITUS. Well, there was an Italian farmer who wanted a box of soil from Italy.

SAMUEL. Just dirt!

LILY BELLE. Mother spent two hundred dollars to get it for him.

TITUS. And there was a flower peddler who asked for a tombstone for his horse.

SAMUEL. He got it.

LILY BELLE. After Father died, this obsession got progressively worse. Last summer she chartered a ship to send a thousand school children around the world.

DR. EMMETT. Why?

TITUS. She said they ought to go around the world while there was still a world around.

LILY BELLE. We stopped her just as she was on the verge of setting up this Fund legally.

SAMUEL. With a board of directors.

LILY BELLE. With a fantastic board of directors. Not a banker, a bishop, or a lawyer among them.

DR. EMMETT. Whom did she choose?

TITUS. A postman—a gardener—a veterinarian—and herself.

LILY BELLE. We should have known her mind was going the day she decided to go on the stage.

TITUS. *(Groans.)* That! Have you ever heard of such a case before, Doctor? What would make a woman of her age suddenly decide to become an actress?

DR. EMMETT. The unique is routine here, Senator. Nothing surprises us.

LILY BELLE. If she had been talented, or even vain—I could have understood it.

TITUS. But she wasn't—she was always quiet—even timid. Then suddenly this amazing change.

SAMUEL. Grief did it.

TITUS. But why turn to acting? Life has enough drama in it.

SAMUEL. God knows.

TITUS. Isn't that right, Doctor?

DR. EMMETT. As Judge Savage says—God knows.

TITUS. And I wish you could explain that bear to us.

DR. EMMETT. Obvious exhibitionism.

TITUS. Exactly.

LILY BELLE. She took a childish delight in being seen everywhere with that teddy bear.

TITUS. Anything to indulge this sudden love for notoriety.

LILY BELLE. Her entire conduct was a travesty of dignity and self-respect.

SAMUEL. And sound business.

DR. EMMETT. Can you tell me, Senator, has there ever been a similar pattern of behavior in your mother's family?

TITUS. Frankly, I don't know.

LILY BELLE. You see, Doctor, she is not actually our mother. Father remarried when we were children.

DR. EMMETT. Oh, I see.

TITUS. But it has never made any difference in our feeling toward her.

DR. EMMETT. Well, I'm afraid I can't be of much help to you until I've had time to observe her conduct here.

TITUS. *(Lightly.)* You're the doctor.

LILY BELLE. And we know she'll be comfortable in such a charming place.

SAMUEL. *(With a nervous laugh.)* I wouldn't mind staying here myself.

TITUS. This is no place to laugh, Samuel.

DR. EMMETT. But we encourage laughter here, Senator—we think it healthy.

TITUS. You do?

DR. EMMETT. Definitely—it's good therapy. For, as Byron says, "And if I laugh at any mortal thing—'Tis that I may not weep."

TITUS. Of course—of course. *(He laughs. Miss Willie enters and stands at door.)*

DR. EMMETT. Yes, Miss Willie?

MISS WILLIE. I beg your pardon, Doctor Emmett, but Doctor Johnson won't be able to complete Mrs. Savage's file for the moment.

DR. EMMETT. Why not?

MISS WILLIE. He finds her a little—uncooperative.

DR. EMMETT. Then bring her in here, please.

MISS WILLIE. Yes, Doctor. *(Goes out.)*

DR. EMMETT. While you're saying goodbye, I'll have a talk with Doctor Johnson.

LILY BELLE. *(Quickly.)* Please don't go, Doctor.

SAMUEL. Please, Doctor.

TITUS. We'd prefer you stayed. I think the shorter we make this, the better for all concerned.

SAMUEL. She's vindictive.

LILY BELLE. For some reason, Doctor, she holds me responsible.

TITUS. We'll have to give her a little more time to get over her resentment. *(Door opens and Miss Willie steps inside. Turns to the door.)*

MISS WILLIE. Will you come in here, Mrs. Savage? *(A pause. It is a long pause while all wait expectantly. Then Mrs. Savage enters. She is diminutive and fragile. It is difficult to judge her exact age from her appearance. Her small, pert face is rather youthful. Her eyes are bright and clear. She wears a constant half-smile which gives the impression of amusement even in anger. Her white hair has been tinted blue and she wears it becomingly arranged. Her dress is too youthful and her feathered hat is capricious. She carries a large teddy bear somewhat the worse for wear. She stands looking around the room appraisingly.)*

DR. EMMETT. *(Indicating a specific chair.)* Will you sit down, Mrs. Savage? *(Mrs. Savage crosses past to another chair and sits down with the bear on her lap. The group watch her silently. She begins to hum to herself.)*

LILY BELLE. We waited to say goodbye to you, Mother.

MRS. SAVAGE. *(Turns and looks at Lily Belle.)*
    I do not like thee, Lily Belle,
    The reason why, I cannot tell;
    But this I know and know full well,
    I do not like thee, Lily Belle.

LILY BELLE. *(Turns to Dr. Emmett.)* She's been chanting that over and over all the way down here.

DR. EMMETT. Your children are leaving, Mrs. Savage. Wouldn't you like to say goodbye to them? *(Mrs. Savage crosses up to window and stands with her arms embracing the bear.)* They would like to say goodbye to you, Mrs. Savage.

MRS. SAVAGE. The fireflies are out. How lovely. *(Turns to Dr. Emmett.)* What makes the fireflies light up, Doctor? Are they mating?

DR. EMMETT. I really couldn't say, Mrs. Savage.

MRS. SAVAGE. I thought you'd know. Isn't this a bug house?

DR. EMMETT. *(Smiles.)* This is "The Cloisters." This is to be your home. I am Doctor Emmett.

MRS. SAVAGE. Wouldn't it be fascinating if human beings glowed like fireflies while they were mating? Do you light up when you're mating, Lily Belle? Lord knows you're flighty.

LILY BELLE. *(Starts for door.)* We might as well go, Titus. She's going to be unpleasant again.

TITUS. Surely, Mother, you're not going to let us depart in an atmosphere of bitterness?

MRS. SAVAGE.
Fifty needles
And fifty pins
And fifty dirty
Republi-kins.
(Turns her back on Titus and looks out window again.)

TITUS. She's determined to take the wrong attitude.

SAMUEL. It's futile.

TITUS. Well—time will take care of this. Come, Samuel.

LILY BELLE. *(Crossing to door.)* I'll send more of her clothes down later, Doctor—we couldn't pack but one grip under the circumstances.

DR. EMMETT. Well, Sunday is visitors' day—if you'd care to bring them down then.

TITUS. My sister is returning to Paris next week, but we'll make arrangements. Good night, Mother. *(They go out.)*

DR. EMMETT. *(Turns to Mrs. Savage.)* If there's anything you need, Mrs. Savage—Miss Wilhelmina will take care of you. *(He follows others out—the door clicks behind him. Mrs. Savage continues to stare out window with her back to Miss Willie. For the first time she becomes aware of confinement. She bows her head and presses her handkerchief to her mouth. Miss Willie crosses to her.)*

MISS WILLIE. We've a lovely garden out there—you'll be able to see it in the morning. *(Mrs. Savage does not answer.)* When I was a child—we always said—*thirty* needles and thirty pins. You've added twenty more dirty Republi-kins.

MRS. SAVAGE. *(Looks up—smiles and turns to Miss Willie.)* It's a fault of mine—exaggeration. It's stupid of me to try to irritate them like this—I just irritate myself. Well, I suppose it has to be exasperating now to be funny later. *(She crosses down to sofa and deposits her bear on a pillow beside her.)*

MISS WILLIE. *(Continues affably.)* I notice one of its eyes is gone.

It must have dropped out in the office. I'll look as soon as they go.

MRS. SAVAGE. Don't bother. It fell out last fall at the opera. I'd have found it but the usher was so nasty about my lighting matches during the Magic Fire music. *(She looks from the bear to Miss Willie.)* You know what this is, don't you?

MISS WILLIE. *(Hesitates.)* Suppose you tell me.

MRS. SAVAGE. It's a teddy bear. Surely you've seen one before?

MISS WILLIE. Not that big.

MRS. SAVAGE. Do you know what I do with it?

MISS WILLIE. I couldn't possibly guess.

MRS. SAVAGE. I sleep with it.

MISS WILLIE. Do you?

MRS. SAVAGE. Yes, I do you. Are you going to talk to me as if I were an imbecile, too?

MISS WILLIE. Here—here—we mustn't be hostile. *(Sits in chair facing Mrs. Savage.)*

MRS. SAVAGE. Of course not—you haven't harmed me. Would you care to know why I sleep with it?

MISS WILLIE. If you'd care to tell me.

MRS. SAVAGE. I don't care. And I'll tell you. I get lonely. I'm too old to have a lover and too fastidious to sleep with a cat.

MISS WILLIE. Then, by all means, you must take it to bed with you here. Would you care to take off your hat?

MRS. SAVAGE. If I'm going to spend the rest of my life here—I might as well. *(Takes it off.)*

MISS WILLIE. It's a mighty saucy hat.

MRS. SAVAGE. A ten-cent piece of felt and three chicken feathers. Eighty-five dollars. Why economy should be expensive—I don't know.

MISS WILLIE. It takes imagination.

MRS. SAVAGE. And the blood of pirates. But I wanted it. I wanted a hat like this since I was sixteen. For all the good it does me now. *(Strokes the feathers fondly.)* Well—I won't need a hat here. *(She holds the hat out.)* Maybe you can use it for something—I'm not at all sure what.

MISS WILLIE. Oh, you'd better keep it. You might need it.

MRS. SAVAGE. *(Sees herself in mirror on L. wall.)* Dear, dear! My hair looks like the matted end of a coconut. *(Crosses to mirror.)*

MISS WILLIE. Oh, I don't think so. It's a heavenly color.

MRS. SAVAGE. *(Brightens.)* You should have seen it last year. *(She laughs.)* It was bright red. Then just to be different, I dyed it black with a white streak in the middle. I looked like nothing so much as a skunk. Finally, I just gave up and tinted it blue. It goes with everything.

MISS WILLIE. It'll certainly go with your room. Wouldn't you like to go up and get settled?

MRS. SAVAGE. Is it time to lock me up?

MISS WILLIE. I wouldn't dream of locking you up. Did you bring a suitcase?

MRS. SAVAGE. My daughter did. I wasn't consulted.

MISS WILLIE. I'll get it and take you up. There'll be time to explore your surroundings tomorrow. *(Starts for door and Mrs. Savage follows her.)* You can wait here.

MRS. SAVAGE. Alone?

MISS WILLIE. Of course.

MRS. SAVAGE. No handcuffs?

MISS WILLIE. We have the honor system. *(Unlocks door L. and goes out. Mrs. Savage goes up to C. windows and tests iron grillwork.)*

MRS. SAVAGE. Honor system, indeed! *(Slowly the sliding doors behind her pull apart and the curious faces of Hannibal, Fairy, Florence, Mrs. Paddy and Jeff appear. Mrs. Savage senses their presence and turns her head to glance behind her. Before she catches sight of her observers, the doors are pushed together with a resounding bang. She crosses C. after a moment, doors slowly part again, and the group enters silently.)*

HANNIBAL. Hello.

FLORENCE. Miss Willie says the bars are only there to keep the world outside.

FAIRY. Corny—isn't it? *(As they cross down C., Fairy comes face to face with Mrs. Savage's teddy bear on sofa. She halts abruptly.)* Oh. *(She backs away.)* It's alive!

FLORENCE. Now, Fairy—you must stop frightening yourself!

MRS. SAVAGE. The poor thing's quite harmless.

FAIRY. It won't bite?

MRS. SAVAGE. It won't shed, lay eggs or bark. And—to the best of my knowledge—it's unvexed by sex. *(Crosses down to bear and pats it.)* It couldn't be less trouble.

FAIRY. In that case any friend of yours is a friend of mine.

FLORENCE. Perhaps we should introduce ourselves. You must be Mrs. Savage. I'm Florence Williams. *(Offers her hand.)*

MRS. SAVAGE. How do you do?

FLORENCE. We have been expecting you all afternoon. We're so glad to have you with us. May I introduce Fairy May?

FAIRY. *(Fervently.)* Say you love me.

MRS. SAVAGE. But—we've just met.

FAIRY. You don't have to mean it. I feel wonderful when people say they love me.

MRS. SAVAGE. Well, I'm sure everyone loves you.

FAIRY. *(Gaily, to the others.)* You see—I told you she wouldn't be spoiled. *(Then to Mrs. Savage.)* Welcome to The Cloisters. Climate best by government test.

MRS. SAVAGE. Thank you.

FLORENCE. And this is Hannibal. *(He bows.)* And this is our Mrs. Paddy.

MRS. SAVAGE. How do you do, Mrs. Paddy? *(Extends her hand. Mrs. Paddy stares at it without expression.)*

MRS. PADDY. I hate everything in the world but most of all I hate lightning, skunk cabbage, custard, mustard, spiders, blisters, girdles, mice, bees, keys, ragweed, chloroform, rhubarb, barnacles, bats, broken glass, eels, crumbs, drunks, tombstones, gallstones, salt, and thunder.

MRS. SAVAGE. *(Blinks and looks at her a moment.)* Why don't you like rhubarb?

HANNIBAL. Mrs. Paddy won't answer you, Mrs. Savage. She'll only recite the things she hates.

FAIRY. Sweet but stubborn.

FLORENCE. Mrs. Paddy stopped talking about twenty years ago.

MRS. SAVAGE. Why?

FAIRY. She got mad.

FLORENCE. Her husband told her to shut up.

FAIRY. And she did.

HANNIBAL. She gave up conversation for life.

FAIRY. But she is only giving up electricity for Lent.

MRS. SAVAGE. *(Takes Mrs. Paddy's hand and pats it.)* You're a woman of wisdom, Mrs. Paddy. There is only one thing wiser than saying very little and that's saying nothing at all. *(Mrs. Paddy reaches over and timidly strokes bear.)* Would you like to hold it? *(Mrs. Paddy quickly picks it up and scurries across to her easel, where she sits quietly—with her arms enfolding the bear and her cheek resting against its fur.)*

FAIRY. She likes you.

MRS. SAVAGE. I like her.

FLORENCE. *(Looks around and sees Jeff standing in background.)* Oh—you haven't met Jeff. Come here, Jeff.

JEFF. *(Puts his R. hand to the side of his face as he comes down to them.)* Please excuse my left hand.

MRS. SAVAGE. Certainly. Is it a toothache?

FLORENCE. *(Placing her arm around Jeff.)* Jeff's face is scarred and he likes to spare people.

MRS. SAVAGE. Well, you don't need to spare me. I have to look at myself every morning.

JEFF. Doctor Emmett refuses to let me wear a bandage.

MRS. SAVAGE. Well, we have to humor our doctors once in a while.

HANNIBAL. And now you have met everyone. We are a small group in this wing and we hope you find us comfortable to be with.

FAIRY. But Mrs. Savage *hasn't* met everyone. She hasn't met the Holy Terror.

HANNIBAL. Of course. How stupid of me.

FAIRY. Where is he, Florence?

FLORENCE. Well, he was here a few moments ago. *(Turns and calls.)* John Thomas!

JEFF. He might have gone out into the hall.

FLORENCE. I'll see. *(Dashes into hallway and disappears for a moment.)* John Thomas!

FAIRY. *(Quickly to Mrs. Savage.)* You won't hurt her, will you?

MRS. SAVAGE. Gracious! Why should I?

JEFF. You won't object, will you?

MRS. SAVAGE. Well—what is John Thomas?

HANNIBAL. Her son. What did you think?

MRS. SAVAGE. Here?

FAIRY. Oh, yes. He was born here.

FLORENCE. *(Returns.)* I can't… *(She stops—smiles—and points behind sofa.)* Oh, look! Asleep on the floor. *(She comes down behind sofa.)* My husband warned me I'd be a bad mother. *(Reaches down behind sofa and picks up a doll dressed in a denim romper.)* Mrs. Savage—this is my son.

FAIRY. *(Quickly.)* You like children, don't you?

MRS. SAVAGE. Everyone's but my own. *(Looking slowly from one to the other before speaking.)* How—old is he?

FLORENCE. Five.

MRS. SAVAGE. He's big for five months.

FLORENCE. No. No. Five years.

MRS. SAVAGE. I meant years.

FLORENCE. Will you excuse me now? I have to put him to bed. *(Walks to door.)* He has measles—I do hope you won't catch them. Excuse me. *(Goes out.)*

JEFF. That was exceedingly kind of you, Mrs. Savage—not to notice anything wrong.

FAIRY. There wasn't time to explain. But you were like lightning.

HANNIBAL. Poor Florence isn't well. We pretend for her sake. We hope you will, too.

MRS. SAVAGE. Oh—I will.

HANNIBAL. I think you should understand right away, Mrs. Savage, that, except for Florence, the rest of us are free to leave here any time we want to.

JEFF. But we don't go—because there's no better place to go.

FAIRY. You're a very lucky woman to be accepted, Mrs. Savage, if I do say it myself. And I do. *(A small buzzer rings on wall above door L. It rings insistently. They all turn toward it with varying degrees of disdain.)*

HANNIBAL. Oh, do be quiet.

FAIRY. Tyrant!

MRS. SAVAGE. What is that?

JEFF. That rude noise is the signal for us to go to our rooms.

HANNIBAL. It's the evil of the machine age. Perfect pistons and no manners.

JEFF. Well—"Ours not to reason why—" *(Stops.)* I wonder why no one ever quotes the first line. It's "Someone blundered." *(Starts out.)*

MRS. SAVAGE. Good night.

JEFF. *(Turns at door.)* I didn't hear you. We never say that. It means there's no more. *(Goes out quickly without explaining.)*

MRS. SAVAGE. *(To Fairy.)* No more what?

FAIRY. *(Airily.)* Oh—there's no more of so much.

HANNIBAL. Don't let Jeff's manner disturb you. During the war his plane was shot down in flames. He hasn't quite recovered yet.

MRS. SAVAGE. Was his face badly burned?

HANNIBAL. Oh, not at all. Jeff bailed out. But he was the only one. He lost his crew. His scar goes deeper than we can see.

FAIRY. Surely you've guessed by now that Hannibal and I are the only guests here free to leave. We couldn't tell you that in front of the others—we pretend, to save their pride. *(Mrs. Paddy rises from behind her easel with an indignant snort. With head held high, she puts bear down and stalks from room. Fairy rushes ahead to guard light switch.)* I'm *sorry*, Mrs. Paddy. I'd forgotten you were still here. I didn't mean *you*, anyhow. *(Mrs. Paddy continues haughtily out of room. Fairy turns to Mrs. Savage.)* Oh, I could tear my tongue out.

Will you excuse me? If I don't apologize, she'll sulk. *(Dashes out after Mrs. Paddy.)*

HANNIBAL. Fairy has the gift of the good for saying the wrong thing.

MRS. SAVAGE. I should think it would take a bit of doing to apologize to someone who won't talk and sulks anyhow.

HANNIBAL. You'll get used to Mrs. Paddy. Just treat her like a clock. Look at her to see how the day goes but don't expect an answer. She's happy at her easel.

MRS. SAVAGE. Is she an artist?

HANNIBAL. I don't know whether she is an artist or not. But she paints.

MRS. SAVAGE. Portraits?

HANNIBAL. Seascapes. Which is rather odd because she's never seen the ocean.

FAIRY. *(Reenters at door briefly.)* I forgot to warn you, Mrs. Savage. Stay awake. If you go to your room—*don't sleep! (Disappears as quickly as she reappeared.)*

MRS. SAVAGE. *(Turns back to Hannibal.)* What did she mean about not sleeping?

HANNIBAL. None of us sleeps here.

MRS. SAVAGE. Where do you sleep?

HANNIBAL. We don't. Oh—we go to our rooms. We've all agreed to that in principle. But we stay awake. We never close our eyes. *(Explains as if to a child.)* When you go to sleep—today ends. And when today ends—tomorrow begins. Today we're safe. Tomorrow may be filled with disaster. *(Brightly.)* You won't catch us sleeping. Could anything be simpler?

MRS. SAVAGE. Not—much.

HANNIBAL. Today's the only certainty.

MISS WILLIE. *(Enters carrying Mrs. Savage's suitcase.)* Hannibal— you heard the buzzer—why aren't you in your room?

HANNIBAL. I am in spirit. And *everyone* says it's the spirit that counts. *(Then to Mrs. Savage.)* Remember—fight the night. *(Goes out quickly.)*

MISS WILLIE. Did they *all* come in to meet you?

MRS. SAVAGE. Well—there was a Mrs. Paddy, and four others who have no business being here at their age.

MISS WILLIE. I quite agree.

MRS. SAVAGE. Do you think *I* belong here?

MISS WILLIE. We're understaffed, Mrs. Savage. I'm kept too busy to have any opinions.

MRS. SAVAGE. I'd like to know what they told you about me.

MISS WILLIE. Was there anything to tell?

MRS. SAVAGE. Did they mention my Memorial Fund?

MISS WILLIE. Not to me.

MRS. SAVAGE. Then they probably told you that my husband's death affected—my reason.

MISS WILLIE. That would be understandable.

MRS. SAVAGE. But untrue.

MISS WILLIE. Why—weren't you happy with your husband?

MRS. SAVAGE. I married Jonathan when I was sixteen. I loved him from the moment I met him until the moment he died. Do you know what that meant?

MISS WILLIE. I think so.

MRS. SAVAGE. Well, you don't, my dear. It meant that my only aim in life was to make him happy—to want what he wanted—to anticipate what would please him. And that meant that all the other things I ever wanted had to be forgotten.

MISS WILLIE. But surely you had no regrets.

MRS. SAVAGE. None. While he lived. But after he was gone—I remembered all the foolish things I'd always wanted to do.

MISS WILLIE. What had you always wanted to do?

MRS. SAVAGE. Things that would have shocked poor Jonathan.

MISS WILLIE. Such as dying your hair blue?

MRS. SAVAGE. That. And studying French. And ballet dancing—and people. As a girl, I was sure I could have been a great actress. So, with no responsibilities and time running out—I decided to be one.

MISS WILLIE. But don't you think you waited too long, Mrs. Savage?

MRS. SAVAGE. I certainly do. Had I been a fool in my youth—no one would have noticed the difference in my old age.

MISS WILLIE. Oh—I'd never think of you as old, Mrs. Savage.

MRS. SAVAGE. Well, having kicked over the traces myself—and learned once again the importance of unimportant things—I decided I'd help others have the foolish things they'd always wanted.

MISS WILLIE. How were you going to do that?

MRS. SAVAGE. By establishing the Jonathan Savage Memorial Fund—a foundation for giving money away in memory of my husband. And that insane idea has brought me here.

MISS WILLIE. Well, you won't find it too unpleasant here. *(Rises.)* Shall we go up to your room now? *(Picks up Mrs. Savage's grip and starts for door.)*

MRS. SAVAGE. Well, at least I learned one thing from my French lessons. *(Crosses to pick up teddy bear on window seat.)*

MISS WILLIE. What's that?

MRS. SAVAGE. What I am. I'm a "mort canard." That's a "dead duck"—I think.

MISS WILLIE. Now it's not as bad as that.

MRS. SAVAGE. Yes, it is. Some day you'll realize that a great injustice was done me. You'll know that I was always quite sane. But here I am—and here they'll try to keep me—with my few foolish years taken from me. *(Miss Willie goes to door R. and stands waiting. Mrs. Savage starts toward door, but instead of crossing in a direct line, she follows the edge of the carpet until it leads her up to Miss Willie. She looks up brightly.)* If people would walk around the edge of the carpet once in a while, it would save wearing it out in the middle. *(She goes out as)*

THE CURTAIN FALLS

Scene 2

TIME: *The next morning.*

AT RISE: *Hannibal stands in c. of room playing his violin. His music consists of only two notes, sawed monotonously on a single string. Fairy sits on floor at Hannibal's feet swaying to the imaginary rhythm. Mrs. Paddy is silent and intent upon her work behind easel. Florence sits on sofa. Turns to doll beside her and puts a warning finger to her lips. Jeffrey sits to L. of Hannibal listening with rapt attention. Mrs. Savage comes to door carrying her bear. She stands on threshold looking from Hannibal to his listeners. The violin noises cease with a flourish from Hannibal's bow.*

FLORENCE. *(Applauding.)* Beautiful—beautiful! What would we do without you, Hannibal? You bring melody to the morning.

JEFF. You could be in the concert field, Hannibal—if you worked at it.

FAIRY. Oh, you're so right, Jeff. Golden fingertips. *(Still carried away.)* I simply surrender to it. I'm a rag.

FLORENCE. *(Turns and sees Mrs. Savage.)* Do come in, Mrs. Savage.

JEFF. I trust you had a pleasant sleepless night?

MRS. SAVAGE. Lovely, thank you. Not a wink.

FLORENCE. You've just missed Hannibal's recital.

MRS. SAVAGE. I heard it. As a matter of fact, it's what brought me out of my room.

FLORENCE. You wouldn't believe it, Mrs. Savage, but Hannibal never touched a violin until last year.

MRS. SAVAGE. What makes you think I wouldn't believe it, my dear? *(Props teddy bear on sofa.)* Was it something you composed yourself, Hannibal?

HANNIBAL. Bach. With variations of my own.

FAIRY. Mathematics' loss was certainly our gain.

MRS. SAVAGE. Now, I don't quite follow that, Fairy.

HANNIBAL. Fairy knows that I used to be a statistician.

MRS. SAVAGE. Thank you—now I'm straight. (Sits c.)

FAIRY. Give him a fraction to multiply.

MRS. SAVAGE. I'm afraid I wouldn't know whether he was right or not.

HANNIBAL. My last position was with the government, charting trends. I was supposed to keep my finger on the pulse of the public and my ear to the ground.

MRS. SAVAGE. A rather vulnerable position, was it not?

HANNIBAL. Very. I was fired and replaced by an electronic calculator.

MRS. SAVAGE. I should think you'd hate electricity, too.

HANNIBAL. No—but I did want to make money with my brains. So I spent the next two years trying to think of something that could be made for a dime—sold for a dollar—and was habit-forming. (Crosses to put violin on piano.) I'm afraid my education was wasted.

FLORENCE. I'm going to send John Thomas to Princeton. Their boys aren't very bright, but they're such gentlemen.

FAIRY. Oh! That reminds me. May we ask you a personal question, Mrs. Savage?

MRS. SAVAGE. They're the only ones worth asking, my dear.

FLORENCE. A little bird told us that you used to be an actress. We're bursting with curiosity. Is it true?

MRS. SAVAGE. Oh—that. Well, if being on the stage makes you an actress—then I guess it's true.

FAIRY. Miss Willie—she's the bird Florence mentioned—told us that you'd been on the New York stage.

HANNIBAL. I wonder if we've ever seen you, Mrs. Savage?

MRS. SAVAGE. Not unless you were quick. Actually I was only in two plays. The first was *Macbeth*.

FAIRY. Oh, I adore *Macbeth*. All that blood. I sent a pint of my blood to the Red Cross once. They sent it back.

JEFF. I should think you would have been a novel departure as Lady Macbeth.

MRS. SAVAGE. I can't tell you how much I agree with you—but they cast me as a witch.

FAIRY. But you're a perfect witch!

MRS. SAVAGE. Thank you, dear.

FAIRY. Please speak some witch talk for us.

MRS. SAVAGE. I didn't have any lines. If I had it probably would have cost me twice as much.

JEFF. Why did it cost you *anything*?

MRS. SAVAGE. I backed the show. If I hadn't put up the money—I couldn't have played even the mute witch. But we made history. It's the first play that ever closed *before* the reviews were out.

FAIRY. Was it expensive?

MRS. SAVAGE. Extremely—but worth it.

FLORENCE. What a pity. Weren't you discouraged?

MRS. SAVAGE. Bitterly. But man is by nature optimistic. If he weren't he'd eat his young. So I decided I'd write a play and star myself.

FAIRY. *(Stops—aghast.)* You wrote a play!

MRS. SAVAGE. I did indeed. With a courage born of ignorance and a plot out of wedlock.

FLORENCE. What part did you play then?

MRS. SAVAGE. Naturally—the lead. *(With a sweep of her hand.)* Not Guilty—starring Ethel P. Savage.

JEFF. What does the "P" stand for?

MRS. SAVAGE. I haven't the faintest idea. My numerologist said I needed it in my name for luck. He was right. We ran a year.

FAIRY. What was the play about?

MRS. SAVAGE. A mother who'd murdered a man and was defended by a young woman lawyer who turns out to be her own daughter. I had red hair and died in my daughter's arms every night and two matinees a week just as the curtain came down and the jury whispered—"Not Guilty." *(Rises to her own applause.)* Oh, I've never had a better time in my life.

HANNIBAL. I gather the notices were good that time?

MRS. SAVAGE. Well, they were sincere. But it didn't make any difference.

FLORENCE. What did they say?

MRS. SAVAGE. The *Times* said my play set the theatre back fifty years. It couldn't possibly—because I stole the plot from *Madame X*, and that's only forty years old.

FAIRY. Wouldn't you think they'd know?

MRS. SAVAGE. But the *Wall Street Journal* was wonderful. It said I brought something new to the theatre.

FAIRY. Money?

FLORENCE. Oh, Fairy—really! Money isn't new.

JEFF. What did Wall Street say?

MRS. SAVAGE. It said I had a "tenacious mediocrity unhampered by taste."

JEFF. But that wasn't good.

MRS. SAVAGE. It was perfect. In our ads we simply said "Tenacious" and "Unhampered."

JEFF. And you ran a year?

MRS. SAVAGE. We'd have been running yet if my daughter hadn't come home and stopped me. Oh, I know I was bad and audiences only came to laugh at me. But we both had a good time. What more can you ask? I do miss it. *(Sighs.)* Oh, well. *(Crosses to reading table L.)* My turn is coming.

FAIRY. I don't think it was very nice of your daughter. *(Then, seeing Mrs. Savage pick up a newspaper, she leaps to her feet and points.)* Don't! Don't do it. Please don't!

FLORENCE. Fairy—what is wrong?

FAIRY. Look—Mrs. Savage is going to read the newspaper. *(Everyone in the room is alerted. Even Mrs. Paddy rises from behind her easel. Mrs. Savage faces them a little apprehensively takes a step backward.)*

FLORENCE. Oh—oh!

MRS. SAVAGE. What's—the matter? *(Jeff followed by Fairy, Hannibal, and Florence all cross quickly to Mrs. Savage.)*

HANNIBAL. I wouldn't do that if I were you, Mrs. Savage.

FLORENCE. Please give it to me. Please—Mrs. Savage.

JEFF. You mustn't read it.

FAIRY. It will only make you unhappy.

MRS. SAVAGE. *(Backs away.)* Now just a moment. I know what the paper is going to say so there is nothing you can hide from me. I've just been waiting for it to happen. *(They look at each other, puzzled.)*

HANNIBAL. Waiting for what to happen, Mrs. Savage?

MRS. SAVAGE. Why—why, what it says in the paper.

JEFF. But we don't know what it says in the paper.

MRS. SAVAGE. Then why were you trying to keep me from seeing it?

HANNIBAL. We have an agreement.

JEFF. We never read the newspapers until they're a month old.

FLORENCE. We find we're much happier when we wait.

MRS. SAVAGE. What are you waiting for?

FAIRY. Why, naturally we're waiting for— *(Turns to Hannibal.)* What do we wait for, Hannibal?

HANNIBAL. Ah—ah—perspective.

JEFF. Peace of mind.

FLORENCE. Security.

JEFF. We believe it's better to read about unpleasant things a month after they've happened.

HANNIBAL. It's reassuring when you know it's over and nothing can be done.

MRS. SAVAGE. My dear people—there is something important in the paper that I want to know about. And I'd like to know now—not next month.

FLORENCE. We're only trying to help you.

FAIRY. Yes!

JEFF. Disaster is easier to digest when it's aged a little.

MRS. SAVAGE. You're very kind but I've made my bed and I want to know who's in it.

FLORENCE. *(To the others.)* We can't prevent Mrs. Savage from reading the paper if she insists. We don't know her well enough to be rude.

HANNIBAL. Florence is right.

FAIRY. Well—if you read anything unpleasant—don't tell us.

GUESTS. *(Together.)* No! *(They move away from Mrs. Savage as if she were about to open Pandora's box and release a host of new apprehensions.)*

FLORENCE. If there's trouble in the world—it won't help us to know about it. *(They stand back and wait while Mrs. Savage searches the pages of the paper.)*

MRS. SAVAGE. This is *yesterday's* paper. *(Looks through other newspapers.)* I want today's paper.

HANNIBAL. Oh, it isn't here yet.

MRS. SAVAGE. When does it come?

HANNIBAL. I don't know.

MRS. SAVAGE. Is there a radio here?

JEFF. Yes—right over there. *(Points to window seat.)*

MRS. SAVAGE. *(Hurries over to it.)* Maybe I can catch the news. *(Switches on radio.)* Why didn't someone mention there was a radio here?

JEFF. You didn't ask us.

MRS. SAVAGE. This doesn't light up. Is anything wrong with the set?

FAIRY. I don't think so. Of course, it hasn't any tubes.

MRS. SAVAGE. It hasn't any—what?

FLORENCE. Tubes. Mrs. Paddy steals them. She hates electricity, you know.

JEFF. No one knows where she hides them.

MRS. SAVAGE. Why didn't you say the set had no tubes?

JEFF. You didn't ask us.

MRS. SAVAGE. Oh dear, dear, dear, dear! *(Stands a moment, looking out window.)* How high is that wall?

HANNIBAL. Much too high.

FAIRY. It's easily ten chairs high.

MRS. SAVAGE. And I suppose no one ever leaves that great gate open?

FLORENCE. Don't look beyond the garden, Mrs. Savage. There may be a better place somewhere—but if you give this up to search for it—you may not find it—and lose what you have.

HANNIBAL. You'll like it here after a while.

FAIRY. Except in January—the rooms get a little cold.

FLORENCE. We like *you* already.

MRS. SAVAGE. It isn't that I don't find you—enchanting, but— *(She flounders.)* but you—

FLORENCE. But we what?

FAIRY. Please don't say anything mean. *(Buzzer on wall begins to signal. Mrs. Savage is forgotten as they turn to it.)* Oh, do be still!

FLORENCE. We have to go, Mrs. Savage.

MRS. SAVAGE. But—where?

HANNIBAL. It's Garden Hour.

FLORENCE. We each have a little plot and we plant things. You can plant anything you wish—vegetables or flowers.

FAIRY. Last year I planted bird seed to see what would come up.

FLORENCE. What did come up, Fairy?

FAIRY. Nothing. But it was a rich horticultural experience.

HANNIBAL. There's a beautiful evergreen in the center. At Christmas it has lights on it saying "Merry Christmas—Keep Out."

FLORENCE. *(Waiting at door with rest of group.)* Come with us, Mrs. Savage. I'll show you my delphiniums.

MRS. SAVAGE. No—please go without me. I have some serious thinking to do. I'll just stay here. *(Begins pacing the room—methodically staying on edge of carpet.)*

JEFF. But the buzzer buzzed. One has to obey orders. *(They stop at door and watch Mrs. Savage a moment.)*

HANNIBAL. May I ask why you're doing that, Mrs. Savage?

MRS. SAVAGE. *(Laughs.)* Oh, I believe in wearing a carpet out evenly.

FAIRY. *(Delighted.)* Oh, how prudent. *(Comes back and falls in behind Mrs. Savage.)* I'm going to help you.

MRS. SAVAGE. But don't you have to garden?

FAIRY. This is more constructive.

FLORENCE. *(Falls in behind Fairy.)* I'll help, too. We must all do our share.

MRS. SAVAGE. But I didn't mean to start a procession.

FAIRY. *(To Hannibal and Jeff.)* Come, boys, many feet make light work.

HANNIBAL. *(To Jeff.)* Why not? It's a refreshing change—most women lead us in circles.

FAIRY. Go ahead, Mrs. Savage. We're behind you.

MRS. SAVAGE. But… *(Reluctantly, she leads her followers around carpet.)* I feel like the Pied Piper. *(Miss Willie enters carrying a vase of flowers. Accustomed to anomalous behavior, she crosses and puts vase on a table L. without comment.)*

FAIRY. You step on leaves, Jeff—Hannibal can take buds—Mrs. Savage can have roses—and the rest of us will walk on thorns. Do you know what we're doing, Miss Willie?

MISS WILLIE. Wearing out the carpet evenly.

FAIRY. Oh, someone told you.

MISS WILLIE. Didn't I hear the buzzer ring Garden Hour?

FAIRY. I didn't hear it. I think it's broken.

MISS WILLIE. *(Stands in front of Fairy.)* Fairy—aren't you ashamed?

FAIRY. Oh, I wish I were dead.

MRS. SAVAGE. I'm afraid this is my fault, Miss Willie.

FLORENCE. I didn't feel like gardening anyhow.

MISS WILLIE. But you've worked so hard with your flowers. Do you want them to die, Florence?

FLORENCE. *(Stricken.)* I don't want anything to die. *(Hurries out.)*

FAIRY. *(Explains to Mrs. Savage.)* Oh, that's so true. Florence wouldn't hurt a fly. She catches them and puts them out the window. Flies adore her.

MISS WILLIE. I think we'd all better go out and work in the garden. Fairy—share your seeds with Mrs. Savage. Run along, now. *(All leave quickly. Mrs. Savage remains.)* Aren't you going with them, Mrs. Savage?

MRS. SAVAGE. I wanted to speak to you—alone.

MISS WILLIE. All right. What can I do for you?

MRS. SAVAGE. A great deal. And it might be that I can do a great deal for you.

MISS WILLIE. Are you about to offer me a bribe, Mrs. Savage?

MRS. SAVAGE. *(Pauses.)* How did you guess?

MISS WILLIE. Everyone does—at first.

MRS. SAVAGE. Still, my offer is a little different. I have the money. I'll give you twenty thousand to leave that door open tonight. *(Miss Willie smiles.) Thirty* thousand.

MISS WILLIE. Don't you like us, Mrs. Savage?

MRS. SAVAGE. That's a most irritating answer to a sound business offer, my dear. Forty thousand. You could be free of this place, too.

MISS WILLIE. But I don't want to be free of it.

MRS. SAVAGE. *Fifty* thousand. You could go around the world— see Cairo—Mandalay—the South Pacific.

MISS WILLIE. But I've seen Cairo—I've been to Mandalay and the South Pacific.

MRS. SAVAGE. You have?

MISS WILLIE. I had four years as an army nurse.

MRS. SAVAGE. Still—you should be able to use fifty thousand dollars.

MISS WILLIE. Now where would you get fifty thousand dollars, Mrs. Savage? That's a fortune.

MRS. SAVAGE. Never mind—I can get it. And in the current idiom— fifty thousand is peanuts.

MISS WILLIE. Oh, I believe you—but I'm afraid I have to refuse.

MRS. SAVAGE. Then you leave me no choice but to burn the place down. *(Crosses toward door.)*

MISS WILLIE. Oh, you wouldn't do that.

MRS. SAVAGE. Oh, yes, I would.

MISS WILLIE. Too many people here wouldn't know how to save themselves. You'd think of them first.

MRS. SAVAGE. If you believe I belong here—why are you appealing to my reason?

MISS WILLIE. I wasn't. I was appealing to your emotions.

MRS. SAVAGE. Well, I'm going to get out quickly enough. It's just that bribing you would have been cheaper. Now it'll cost me a couple of million at least. *(She turns and goes out. Miss Willie begins to straighten the room. Dr. Emmett lets himself in at L. and comes down to Miss Willie.)*

MISS WILLIE. Good morning, Doctor.

DR. EMMETT. Good morning. Is Mrs. Savage downstairs?

MISS WILLIE. She just this minute went out to the garden.

DR. EMMETT. What is her state of mind this morning?

MISS WILLIE. The usual pattern. She's already offered me a bribe.

DR. EMMETT. What did she offer you?

MISS WILLIE. *(Laughs.)* The highest yet. Fifty thousand—the poor dear!

DR. EMMETT. Did she sound confident?

MISS WILLIE. Definitely manic. She talked as if she still controlled her own affairs.

DR. EMMETT. Apparently she does. Read this. *(Hands her a newspaper.)* I've just been talking to her children—they're practically out of their minds themselves. The Senator is leaving Washington at once—he'll pick up his sister in New York and the Judge in Boston and be here by tonight.

MISS WILLIE. *(Looks up from paper.)* This is the most amazing story I've ever read. When did they discover it?

DR. EMMETT. I gather this morning. They asked me to confine her to her room.

MISS WILLIE. I don't understand it—how could she get away with so much money?

DR. EMMETT. Apparently her husband left the estate to her. She's been secretly selling out control ever since.

MISS WILLIE. Ten million dollars—that's a typographical error, isn't it?

DR. EMMETT. No, they had it all right.

MISS WILLIE. But what could she have done with it?

DR. EMMETT. As her son says, God knows.

MISS WILLIE. Could she have spent it?

DR. EMMETT. I doubt it. Will you call her, please? I'd better tell her what to expect.

MISS WILLIE. *(Calls out window.)* Oh, Mrs. Savage—would you come in, please? Doctor Emmett wants to see you. *(Turns back to Dr. Emmett.)* Are you going to place her in seclusion?

DR. EMMETT. Of course not. But sometimes I wish there was a way of placing relations in seclusion. They are always much more trouble than patients.

MISS WILLIE. Do you think she knows what happened to the money?

DR. EMMETT. If she does—she's the only one.

MISS WILLIE. Is there any possibility that there's method in her madness?

DR. EMMETT. Miss Willie, I find it harder every day to say exactly where reason ends and madness begins. For the moment I must accept the presumptive evidence of her step-children.

MISS WILLIE. Well—from what I've heard, her son's record in Congress would give any good psychiatrist a nasty turn.

DR. EMMETT. It certainly would—and the sensationalism of her daughter's six divorces doesn't speak too well for her emotional stability, either. *(Before Miss Willie can answer, Mrs. Savage enters.)*

MRS. SAVAGE. Did you want me, Doctor?

DR. EMMETT. Yes. Good morning. *(Turns to Miss Willie.)* Will you help out on the switchboard, Miss Willie? Miriam has been deluged with calls from newspapers.

MISS WILLIE. Yes, Doctor. *(She goes out.)*

DR. EMMETT. Please sit down, Mrs. Savage.

MRS. SAVAGE. *(Sits down.)* I *think* I know what you're going to tell me.

DR. EMMETT. Do you?

MRS. SAVAGE. I see you have the morning papers. I wondered how long it would take them to find out.

DR. EMMETT. Then you're aware of what you've done. And the consequences?

MRS. SAVAGE. Oh, it's too early for consequences. May I see it?

DR. EMMETT. *(Hands her papers, which she reads.)* The Senator phoned from Washington. We can expect them by tonight.

MRS. SAVAGE. Indeed we can. Well, I'm not going any place.

DR. EMMETT. How could you possibly have spent ten million dollars without someone knowing about it!

MRS. SAVAGE. Who said I spent it?

DR. EMMETT. That paper says you did.

MRS. SAVAGE. Oh, what do they know? I didn't spend it—I couldn't. I hid it.

DR. EMMETT. You *hid* it?

MRS. SAVAGE. In nice half-million-dollar negotiable bonds that can't be traced.

DR. EMMETT. Why?

MRS. SAVAGE. I don't ask you what you do with your money, Doctor.

DR. EMMETT. I'm sorry this has happened, Mrs. Savage. I'm afraid your hidden treasure is going to prove a great disadvantage to you.

MRS. SAVAGE. That's because you're a doctor—and doctors never know the value of money.

DR. EMMETT. *(Goes to door L. and stops.)* Would you like to know how long it would take me to earn that much money, Mrs. Savage? *(Before Mrs. Savage can answer, Hannibal comes in R. and picks up his violin.)*

HANNIBAL. Oh—excuse me—I came back to get my violin. Fairy May wants music while she plants her seeds.

DR. EMMETT. Oh—just a moment, Hannibal. You were a statistician—how long would it take the average doctor to earn ten million dollars?

HANNIBAL. *(Quickly.)* Well—he'd have to start before Christ was born and work right through the burning of Rome up to the burning of St. Joan and Savonarola. With time out, of course, for the Norman Conquest, the Crusades, the Hundred Years' War—the Thirty Years' War—and the Seven Years' War. So he'd have to work double-time during the discovery of America, up to penicillin and bubble gum. *But* that's without deducting federal tax—state tax—city tax—school tax—luxury tax and amusement tax. You'd add a hundred years for that.

DR. EMMETT. Thank you, Hannibal. It's a great deal to be responsible for, Mrs. Savage. *(Goes out.)*

HANNIBAL. Now what's the Doctor up to?

MRS. SAVAGE. A bit of emotional blackmail, I suspect. *(Turns to Hannibal.)* Hannibal—would you guess to look at me that I'm worth ten million dollars on the hoof?

HANNIBAL. Never. The human body has only twenty cents' worth of calcium in it—five cents' worth of iodine, twenty cents' worth of phosphorus, and—well—even at present high prices—nobody is worth over a dollar and a half.

MRS. SAVAGE. So you only value me at a dollar and a half?

HANNIBAL. Never. You said "worth." Your *value* is inestimable.

MRS. SAVAGE. Hannibal—I like you. I like you very much. You make me feel important. You make me feel like dancing.

HANNIBAL. Splendid. *(Promptly chins his violin.)* What shall I play?

MRS. SAVAGE. *(Laughs.)* Anything.

HANNIBAL. *(Eagerly.)* I am very good on "The Flight of the Bumble Bee."

MRS. SAVAGE. Could anything be more appropriate—the bees come home and find the honey gone! Someone is going to be stung. *(Raises a hand.)* Play—Hannibal! *(As he begins his two-note sawing of the strings again, Mrs. Savage conducts with enthusiasm.)*

THE CURTAIN FALLS

ACT II

SCENE 1

TIME: *The same night. After dinner.*

AT RISE: *Hannibal, Florence, and Jeff sit at table L., playing cards. Mrs. Paddy sits upstage with her back to audience, facing her canvas. For the first time we are able to look at the seascape she is painting. A single undulating line represents the vast ocean. There is nothing more. Mrs. Savage sits with a book and reading glasses on, downstage R. Fairy May wanders about, sighing intermittently.*

FAIRY. *(Stops beside Mrs. Savage and leans over her shoulder.)* Are you reading?

MRS. SAVAGE. *(Looks up from her book.)* Yes, dear.

FAIRY. *(Walks back to look out window and returns.)* Is it interesting?

MRS. SAVAGE. Very.

FAIRY. I'm not disturbing you, am I?

MRS. SAVAGE. Now what ever makes you think that? *(Fairy sighs and starts away again. Mrs. Savage puts down her book.)* What's the matter, Fairy May?

FAIRY. Nothing. It's just that no one has said they loved me this live-long day.

MRS. SAVAGE. Why, yes, they have, Fairy.

FAIRY. Oh, no they haven't. I've been waiting.

MRS. SAVAGE. I heard Florence say it at the dinner table.

FAIRY. Did she?

FLORENCE. Did I?

MRS. SAVAGE. She said, "Don't eat too fast, Fairy."

FAIRY. Was that saying she loved me?

42

MRS. SAVAGE. Of course. People say it when they say, "Take an umbrella, it's raining"—or "Hurry back"—or even "Watch out, you'll break your neck." There're hundreds of ways of wording it—you just have to listen for it, my dear.

FAIRY. *(Brightening.)* My dentist said I had perfect occlusion. Do you think he was telling me he loved me?

MRS. SAVAGE. What else? Why, the first day I met my husband, I was riding horseback and he said I had a good seat. I knew immediately he loved me.

FAIRY. Oh, thank you. I've been missing so much. Oh! My dentist loves me.

MRS. SAVAGE. Now—what else would you like to have me clear up for you?

FAIRY. Nothing. I'm sorry I disturbed you. Thank you and forgive me. *(Mrs. Savage goes back to her book.)*

FLORENCE. Mrs. Savage?

MRS. SAVAGE. *(Puts down book.)* Yes?

FLORENCE. I'm keeping score and the boys won't help me. What's seven and five and four?

MRS. SAVAGE. Forty-nine.

HANNIBAL. But, Mrs. Savage—

MRS. SAVAGE. It's my own system, Hannibal. I refuse to submit to the tyranny of mathematics. *(Goes back to her book.)*

FLORENCE. Then I win.

HANNIBAL. I'll keep score after this.

FAIRY. *(Comes back to stand beside Mrs. Savage.)* Mrs. Savage?

MRS. SAVAGE. *(Lowers book again.)* Yes, Fairy?

FAIRY. May I interrupt you a moment?

MRS. SAVAGE. Of course.

FAIRY. There *is* one other thing you can clear up for me. Why is it suddenly Sunday again when it was Sunday only yesterday?

MRS. SAVAGE. Why do you think it's Sunday?

FAIRY. If your children are coming to see you—it must be Sunday, because that's visitors' day. I guess I had an awfully good time this week.

MRS. SAVAGE. It isn't Sunday, Fairy. My brood are coming back because they couldn't wait a week.

FAIRY. That should make you happy.

MRS. SAVAGE. It should but it doesn't. *(Puts book down and crosses to card game.)*

FAIRY. Excuse me. Don't you like them?

MRS. SAVAGE. Not at all.

FLORENCE. Oh, I think that's a wicked thing to say.

MRS. SAVAGE. Well, we have to be wicked once in a while to get God's attention. But if it consoles you, Florence—they were not mine. My husband was left with three small children. *(Stands looking over Florence's shoulder.)*

FLORENCE. But you must have liked them when they were little?

MRS. SAVAGE. Oh, I wanted to make them my own, desperately. But they always resented me. Why, the first time I put my arms around Lily Belle, she bit me—and she bit me every day until she was ten.

FAIRY. That must have made you very highstrung.

HANNIBAL. What stopped her at the exact age of ten?

MRS. SAVAGE. I suppose at ten a girl begins to consider her teeth.

FLORENCE. But the boys—boys are always so much better.

MRS. SAVAGE. Not always. They'd been spoiled by money. And whenever I tried to correct them, they'd break something I treasured, to get even with me. It was a happy day when they went away to school.

JEFF. School must have taught them something.

MRS. SAVAGE. Yes—French. After that, whenever they came home, they spoke nothing but French so I couldn't understand them. And I haven't understood them since.

FLORENCE. But you must be proud of them now. The Senator is quite famous, isn't he?

MRS. SAVAGE. That he is—make no mistake. I'm told he gets more threatening telegrams than any other man in Congress. I believe Western Union lists him as a tangible asset.

JEFF. If he's so unpopular, why do the voters keep sending him back to Washington?

MRS. SAVAGE. They're no fools. It's the only way to keep him out of the State.

JEFF. The other son's a judge, isn't he?

FAIRY. That's a distinction.

MRS. SAVAGE. He's made it one. He has the distinction of having had more of his decisions reversed than any man in jurisprudence.

FAIRY. Is the daughter pretty, Mrs. Savage?

MRS. SAVAGE. Well, there's a picture of her in the paper—I'll show it to you and you can judge for yourself. *(Starts for newspaper on sofa.)*

FLORENCE. *(Rises.)* Oh, don't read us anything out of the paper, please.

MRS. SAVAGE. I won't. I'll just show you her picture.

HANNIBAL. *(Rises.)* We don't look at pictures, either.

FLORENCE. People are always pinned under trucks.

FAIRY. I'll peek first to make sure it isn't horrible.

MRS. SAVAGE. *(Folds paper.)* Well—even I don't say it's horrible.

FAIRY. *(Glances at picture and shrieks.)* Oh! She's a queen! She's wearing a crown!

FLORENCE. Oh—a queen?

MRS. SAVAGE. That's a tiara, Fairy. It's an old picture taken when she was married to her Slovak Prince.

JEFF. Let's take a quick look, Hannibal, just to be polite. *(All cross to Mrs. Savage and look.)*

FAIRY. Then she's a princess?

MRS. SAVAGE. No—she discarded the prince a good six husbands ago.

FAIRY. Oh, but why?

MRS. SAVAGE. Hell hath no music like a woman playing second fiddle.

FAIRY. But she kept the tiara?

MRS. SAVAGE. Indeed she did. I suspect she sleeps in it.

FLORENCE. I don't know when I've seen a prettier tiara.

HANNIBAL. The dress is cut rather low, isn't it?

FAIRY. I don't like her. Let's do something mean to her.

FLORENCE. Why, Fairy!

FAIRY. Oh, I don't mean really mean—something like—like putting her picture on the dart board and throwing darts at it.

HANNIBAL. Fairy!

MRS. SAVAGE. My dear—you're a sweet child. That's exactly what we'll do. *(Starts tearing out picture.)*

FLORENCE. Oh, you wouldn't.

MRS. SAVAGE. I need exercise, my dear.

FLORENCE. Fairy—you're an evil girl to think up such a thing.

FAIRY. Don't you talk to me like that—I'm sensitive!

MRS. SAVAGE. Leave her alone, Florence. I'm the culprit. Let's see— now what can I pin it up with?

FAIRY. Mrs. Paddy has some thumbtacks.

FLORENCE. Oh, Fairy, I'm so disappointed in you.

FAIRY. I wish I had died in my cradle.

MRS. SAVAGE. *(Crosses to Mrs. Paddy.)* Mrs. Paddy—that's the loveliest seascape I've ever seen. Do you know, I can actually smell the ocean? *(Mrs. Paddy beams.)* I think your genius lies in your simplicity—you challenge the imagination. *(Mrs. Paddy nods agree- ment.)* Could I borrow four thumbtacks? *(Mrs. Paddy hands her four thumbtacks.)* Thank you. *(Crosses to dart board.)*

FLORENCE. It's setting a very bad example for motherhood.

MRS. SAVAGE. Do stop worrying, Florence. *(Pins the picture on dart board.)* Don't you like surprises?

FLORENCE. Yes.

MRS. SAVAGE. Well, I want to surprise Lily Belle. I'll tee off. *(They gather behind her.)* Now—target for tonight. *(She throws a dart.)* Right in the tiara!

FLORENCE. Something dreadful is going to happen, I know. *(As Mrs. Savage takes out dart, Miss Willie enters.)*

MISS WILLIE. Everybody to the upstairs study. Mrs. Savage's visitors are here.

FAIRY. *(Rushes over to Miss Willie.)* Miss Willie—may I stay? I never meet strangers any more. Please let me.

MISS WILLIE. I'm sorry, Fairy—but the Senator insisted on privacy. Hurry now—everybody out.

FAIRY. *(Following others out.)* Some day when I'm ordered out— I'm just going to go without saying a word. I have as much pride as anyone.

MISS WILLIE. *(Leans into hallway.)* All the way upstairs now. *(Closes sliding doors and crosses back to L.)*

MRS. SAVAGE. How's the weather out there?

MISS WILLIE. *(Smiling.)* Stormy. *(Goes out. Mrs. Savage crosses to desk and picks up a piece of paper. She writes on it hurriedly and, folding note, thrusts it down front of her dress. Goes back C. and tosses another dart. Miss Willie comes in, holding door open.)* Here are your visitors, Mrs. Savage. *(Samuel, Titus, and Lily Belle enter—martyred and angry.)*

LILY BELLE. That will be all. You can wait outside.

MISS WILLIE. *(Takes latch off door.)* I'll leave the latch off and wait at the hall desk. *(Goes out.)*

TITUS. I don't know what to say to you, Mother. For the life of me, I don't know what to say.

MRS. SAVAGE. Polite people say "Good evening."

LILY BELLE. Deception is so unlike you.

SAMUEL. I'm not angry—I'm just hurt.

TITUS. Have you the faintest idea of the enormity of what you've done? You've sold control of fifteen Savage industries.

LILY BELLE. We'll have to sell our stock in Savage Brass to buy it back.

MRS. SAVAGE. Oh, didn't you find out? I sold that first.

LILY BELLE. I mustn't get excited—I mustn't get excited—I get lines. *(Crosses to sofa.)*

TITUS. What else—what else did you dispose of?

MRS. SAVAGE. Everything in my name.

SAMUEL. *(Sits down quickly.)* We're ruined.

TITUS. Where is the money? You couldn't have spent it?

LILY BELLE. Tell us what you did with it, dear?

MRS. SAVAGE. I converted it into a neat little bundle of negotiable bonds—and buried them.

TITUS. When you say "buried"—you mean "hidden"?

MRS. SAVAGE. I mean buried—as in "funeral."

SAMUEL. In the ground?

LILY BELLE. I feel physically ill.

TITUS. Where is it buried?

MRS. SAVAGE. I forget. *(Sits chair c.)*

TITUS. Oh, Lord, grant my mother one moment of clarity!

LILY BELLE. Where did you bury it—concentrate!

MRS. SAVAGE. *(Puffs her cheeks with air, then explodes them.)* Best thing in the world for taking lines out of the face, Lily Belle. *(Turns her attention to teddy bear.)* I've got to do something about getting you a new eye. Do you know any place that sells bears' eyes, Lily Belle?

LILY BELLE. Give me that stupid thing and answer us! *(Tries to take bear away from Mrs. Savage.)*

MRS. SAVAGE. *(Rises.)* Miss Willie! Help!

TITUS. Lily Belle—wait! You're just antagonizing her. We won't get anywhere shouting.

LILY BELLE. I'm sorry, Mother. Hold your bear. We forget that you're sick.

TITUS. *(Strides away from Mrs. Savage.)* What we must make you understand, Mother, is that the money involved is not what concerns us so much as the disgrace of all— *(His speech is interrupted by a scream from Lily Belle. He whirls about.)* What happened?

LILY BELLE. *(Backing away from Mrs. Savage.)* She bit me! *(Rubs her hand and glares at Mrs. Savage, who has recaptured her teddy bear.)*

TITUS. Nonsense. Whatever Mother might do—she wouldn't descend to biting.

SAMUEL. It was a wasp.

LILY BELLE. If ever there was a wasp—it's the woman we call Mother. I know when I'm bitten. *(Holds hand out in evidence.)* *Teeth marks.*

TITUS. *(Softly.)* There is no need to raise your voice.

SAMUEL. Does it hurt?

LILY BELLE. OF COURSE IT HURTS!

TITUS. Lily Belle—we'll get nowhere fighting among ourselves. Now stop it. We can't afford it.

MRS. SAVAGE. You can't afford anything.

TITUS. We simply refuse to be angry with you, Mother. *(Turns to Lily Belle.)* Lily Belle, apologize.

LILY BELLE. I will not.

TITUS. Lily Belle!

LILY BELLE. *(Swallows her pride with a distasteful gulp.)* Mother, it's quite all right. I don't object to your biting me— *(Crosses back to her.)* gnaw and mangle me to the bone—gum me to your heart's content—only tell us what you did with our money.

MRS. SAVAGE. *My* money—you've already had your share.

LILY BELLE. The estate is ours. It's belonged to the Savage family for generations.

SAMUEL. Eight generations.

TITUS. It's unthinkable that you should be the first Savage to be found wanting.

MRS. SAVAGE. Found wanting what?

TITUS. The Savage pride. Now I want you to listen carefully to what I have to say. *(Sits beside her as Lily Belle wanders up toward window.)* The estate has always been a sacred trust. We have never considered ourselves possessors of a great fortune—but custodians of wealth—

LILY BELLE. *(Puts hand to her throat and gives birth to an agonized bleat.)* Oooooooh!

TITUS. *(Leaps to his feet.)* Don't do that!

LILY BELLE. Look! I just ask you to look! She's been throwing darts at my picture!

TITUS. What of it? That can't possibly hurt you.

LILY BELLE. It's a vicarious form of murdering someone. It's just the most vicious sort of voodoo magic known to science.

SAMUEL. We're losing ground.

LILY BELLE. We were fostered by a werewolf—every Savage son of us!

TITUS. My patience is exhausted. *(Turns to Mrs. Savage and shouts.)* What have you done with the money?

MRS. SAVAGE. *(Shouting.)* I told you. I buried it!

TITUS. Where? Unless you tell us at once, you're going to a public institution. We'll not tolerate this criminal waste.

MRS. SAVAGE. You've got me in such a state, I can't think. I haven't a brain in my head, anyhow—you've said so time and again.

SAMUEL. Not me.

MRS. SAVAGE. With all this shouting—you've given me a headache. I can't remember a thing.

TITUS. What do you mean you can't remember a thing? Of course you can.

MRS. SAVAGE. I can't. My head is pounding.

LILY BELLE. We'd better be careful, Titus.

TITUS. *(Alarmed.)* Can we get something for you?

MRS. SAVAGE. Yes—the only thing that clears my head is those powders I used to take.

TITUS. Where are they?

MRS. SAVAGE. I'm out of them.

TITUS. We'll get more.

MRS. SAVAGE. *(Brightly.)* Will you?

TITUS. Of course.

MRS. SAVAGE. *(Takes out folded note.)* Here's the prescription number—it's from my druggist. In Boston.

TITUS. You mean drive all the way back to *Boston*!

MRS. SAVAGE. *(Leans forward and clutches her head.)* Where is everyone?

SAMUEL. Are you ill?

LILY BELLE. Titus—this is dangerous—we'd better get those powders and come back in the morning. We won't accomplish anything tonight.

TITUS. Yes—I agree with you. *(Hands note to Lily Belle.)* You get the prescription filled.

LILY BELLE. *(Immediately hands note to Samuel.)* Get it filled, Samuel—when we get back I'm going right to bed. *(Samuel takes prescription, reads it to himself.)*

TITUS. Are you prepared to tell us what you've done with those bonds in the morning?

MRS. SAVAGE. *(Nods.)* Pound—pound—pound.

SAMUEL. *(Puts note away and hurriedly starts for door.)* I'll tell the chauffeur we're ready. *(Goes out quickly.)*

TITUS. *(Looks after Samuel, puzzled by his speed.)* Now what got into him? Well—we'd better go, then. We'll be back first thing in the morning.

MRS. SAVAGE. *(Looks up vaguely.)* Pound—pound—pound!

TITUS. Come, Lily Belle. I'll have Doctor Emmett give her a sedative. *(Goes out ahead of Lily Belle.)*

MRS. SAVAGE. Lily Belle. Pst!

LILY BELLE. *(Stops.)* What do you mean by—pst?

MRS. SAVAGE. *(Whispers.)* I've something important to tell you about the bonds. Close the door.

LILY BELLE. *(Shuts door and returns to Mrs. Savage.)* Well?

MRS. SAVAGE. I want to tell *you*—and you alone—where I hid them.

LILY BELLE. *(Suspiciously.)* Why me?

MRS. SAVAGE. Titus and Samuel are fools—and if anything happened to me overnight…the bonds would be lost.

LILY BELLE. *(Glances toward door.)* It was Titus who wanted you here—not I. Where did you hide them?

MRS. SAVAGE. Where would *you* hide ten million dollars—if you didn't trust banks?

LILY BELLE. I don't know.

MRS. SAVAGE. Under a rock?

LILY BELLE. Of course not.

MRS. SAVAGE. Would you hide them in your mattress? Of course—you're never far from your mattress—but what if you were, and the house burned down?

LILY BELLE. Are you going to tell me or not?

MRS. SAVAGE. Have you ever been to the Museum of Natural History?

LILY BELLE. No.

MRS. SAVAGE. Very educational. And fireproof.

LILY BELLE. Mother—please! (*Glances uneasily at door.*)

MRS. SAVAGE. Do you know what's on the third floor of the Museum?

LILY BELLE. How could I?

MRS. SAVAGE. The Department of Ichthyology.

LILY BELLE. What *are* you talking about?

MRS. SAVAGE. Fish. In the last room on the third floor—hanging from two wires—is a big dusty porpoise.

LILY BELLE. Well?

MRS. SAVAGE. I stuffed my bonds in that stuffed fish when no one was looking.

LILY BELLE. I don't believe you.

MRS. SAVAGE. Name me a safer place.

LILY BELLE. (*Pacing.*) Only a fool would do such a thing.

MRS. SAVAGE. That's me.

LILY BELLE. (*Suspiciously.*) How could you get a package of bonds inside a porpoise?

MRS. SAVAGE. Easy. A razor blade and scotch tape.

LILY BELLE. How do I know you're telling me the truth?

MRS. SAVAGE. There's a simple way to find out.

LILY BELLE. *(Stops, looks directly at Mrs. Savage and smiles.)* You must think I'm very gullible. I have no intention of hunting inside a stuffed fish. *(Door opens and Titus steps inside.)*

TITUS. Are we to hold the car all night for you, Lily Belle? Samuel is honking.

LILY BELLE. Let him honk. *(Strides past him and goes out.)*

TITUS. Doctor Emmett will see you in a few minutes. *(Turns to go.)*

MRS. SAVAGE. Titus.

TITUS. Yes.

MRS. SAVAGE. Kiss me goodbye?

TITUS. You bit Lily Belle. I don't trust you. *(Turns to go out.)*

MRS. SAVAGE. That's ironical—because I trust you. I was just about to tell you where the bonds are hidden.

TITUS. *(Stops, closes door, and returns.)* Surely you know that I never wanted you here. I listened to Lily Belle.

MRS. SAVAGE. Will you get me out of here—and let me alone?

TITUS. You know I will.

MRS. SAVAGE. Then I'll tell you. The bonds are in a tin box.

TITUS. Where?

MRS. SAVAGE. Do you remember when I went to Washington with a group from Actors' Equity?

TITUS. No.

MRS. SAVAGE. Well, I do. It was National Ethel Week. We all had lunch with the First Lady. There was Ethel Barrymore, Ethel Merman, Ethel Waters, Ethel…

TITUS. What are you talking about!

MRS. SAVAGE. My bonds are buried in the president's hothouse.

TITUS. I don't believe you.

MRS. SAVAGE. You didn't believe Pearl Harbor until you investigated.

TITUS. Why would you choose such a public place—everybody in and out?

MRS. SAVAGE. *(Defensively.)* Well, I'm not very bright.

TITUS. *I'm* the only man who can't get into the White House.

MRS. SAVAGE. You should agree with him oftener.

TITUS. How do I know you didn't imagine this?

MRS. SAVAGE. There's one sure way to find out. Dig.

TITUS. Oh, no. I'm not going to fall into that trap. You didn't bury the box there.

MRS. SAVAGE. In the corner—under the petunia bed. *(Door opens and Lily Belle steps in.)*

LILY BELLE. Titus—unless you hurry, Samuel is going off without us.

TITUS. I'm coming. *(Lily Belle leaves. Titus goes to door and stops to face Mrs. Savage.)* I refuse to believe you. *(Strides out, closing door behind him. He has no sooner left than sliding doors pop open, and Hannibal, Jeff, Florence, Mrs. Paddy, and Fairy come tumbling in.)*

FAIRY. We listened! We're horrible!

FLORENCE. We're quite ashamed.

FAIRY. We *all* wish we were dead.

HANNIBAL. We wanted to stop listening and sneak away, but we couldn't without making too much noise.

MRS. SAVAGE. It's quite all right. It's no secret. If you read the papers you'd know.

FAIRY. *(Brightening.)* Did you *really* hide all that money?

MRS. SAVAGE. I did indeed—for my Memorial Fund.

FLORENCE. And now you're giving it back.

FAIRY. You're very generous for your size and weight.

HANNIBAL. But you didn't tell the Judge where his share was.

MRS. SAVAGE. That prescription was really a note saying to dig under the chimney.

JEFF. But why did you hide it if you were going to tell them where it was?

MRS. SAVAGE. What makes you think I did?

FAIRY. We heard you.

MRS. SAVAGE. Foolish I am—but not that foolish. Whatever is in the chimney, or under the president's petunias, or stuck in that porpoise—I can assure you—it is not my little bundle of bonds.

FAIRY. Then why did you say they were?

MRS. SAVAGE. I want to see to what extent they'll make fools of themselves.

FAIRY. Oh. Nothing makes the truth seem so shabby as a magnificent lie. How splendid!

JEFF. How do you know they'll believe you?

MRS. SAVAGE. They *want* to believe me.

HANNIBAL. They might consider it degrading to go out digging.

MRS. SAVAGE. But they will.

JEFF. How can you be sure?

MRS. SAVAGE. *(Picks up handful of darts.)* There are a million things a man won't do for five dollars—but there aren't five things a man won't do for a million. They'll dig. *(Tosses another dart at dart board, scoring a hit. Others applaud as)*

THE CURTAIN FALLS

SCENE 2

TIME: *A few nights later.*

AT RISE: *Mrs. Savage sits alone on window seat, looking out toward garden. Jeff comes in and looks about without seeing her. Glances down at piano and then behind him into hall to make sure he is alone. Then comes down to piano and stands in front of it. Smiles and rubs his fingers to limber them. Then, seating himself, strikes a chord. Mrs. Savage rises.*

MRS. SAVAGE. Oh! You startled me.

JEFF. *(Quickly rises and covers R. side of his face with his hand.)* I didn't know anyone was in here.

MRS. SAVAGE. And I didn't know you could play the piano. *(Comes down to him.)*

JEFF. I only play when I'm alone.

MRS. SAVAGE. Oh, you shouldn't be so shy. No one is going to compare you with a professional.

JEFF. But I *am* a professional.

MRS. SAVAGE. Oh.

JEFF. I made my debut in Town Hall a week before the war. Jeffrey Meredith. You see? *(Takes clipping from his wallet.)*

MRS. SAVAGE. Why, it says you were brilliant! Forgive me, Jeff. I should have known.

JEFF. *(Smiles.)* I was going to appear with the Philharmonic. I didn't—but I have the contract to prove I might have.

MRS. SAVAGE. But you never play, Jeff. Oh, please go on—I'd like to hear you.

JEFF. *(Puts hand to face again.)* No. I don't like to be stared at.

MRS. SAVAGE. *(Pats him affectionately on shoulder.)* I'll look the other way and listen, Jeff.

JEFF. I'd rather not. I'm not ready to face people yet. Please don't insist.

MRS. SAVAGE. I wouldn't dream of it. *(Sits on sofa.)*

JEFF. Thank you. *(Crosses to sit beside her.)* Can you keep a secret?

MRS. SAVAGE. About ten minutes.

JEFF. Doctor Emmett isn't a doctor at all.

MRS. SAVAGE. What is he?

JEFF. A patient—just like Mrs. Paddy.

MRS. SAVAGE. Oh—do you think so?

JEFF. For five years now he's promised to give me a new face.

MRS. SAVAGE. No, he's a doctor, Jeff. It says so on his office door. He wouldn't lie.

JEFF. Do you believe a man is what he claims to be?

MRS. SAVAGE. I'm a trusting soul. I try to believe the best of people.

JEFF. It's best to believe the worst. If you believe the worst, then the worst is only half bad at best. And the best is no worse than expected. So it's best to believe the worst.

MRS. SAVAGE. *(Ponders this for a moment.)* You know, Jeffrey— that's just obscure enough to be profound. What does it mean?

JEFF. It's simple. When a man says he is wise, you say he's a fool. But if he says he's a fool—you believe him.

MRS. SAVAGE. Well, only a fool claims to be wise.

JEFF. *(Triumphantly.)* Exactly! Which proves I'm right. Doctor Emmett is a fool. He claims he's a doctor. The war was over five years ago—and where's his miracle?

MRS. SAVAGE. Some things take a long time to heal, Jeffrey.

JEFF. I can't wait much longer. I'm getting old. I'll be twenty-six soon.

MRS. SAVAGE. And that's ancient. Why don't you forget your appearance and play, anyhow? Don't condemn your audience before you give them a chance to be kind.

JEFF. Look at me and then tell me an audience won't shudder at the sight of me. *(Rises and stands in front of her with hand covering his face toward audience.)* Look! *(Slowly takes his hand away.)* Do you see?

MRS. SAVAGE. *(Looks at Jeffrey's handsome and unblemished face.)* I see nothing—to hide, Jeffrey.

JEFF. Doctor Emmett told you what to say.

MRS. SAVAGE. No, he didn't, I promise. But I'd trust him if I were you. Give him a little more time.

JEFF. All right. I'll give him five years more.

MRS. SAVAGE. Fair enough.

JEFF. Do you know something?

MRS. SAVAGE. Not a thing. I'm awed only by the magnitude of what I don't know.

JEFF. I wouldn't tell this to anyone else. *(Glances around cautiously.)* Hannibal really can't play the violin.

MRS. SAVAGE. No!

JEFF. Yes!

MRS. SAVAGE. Well, of course, I'm tone deaf.

JEFF. I'll tell you something else. I sometimes wish I were.

MRS. SAVAGE. Well, you're a sweet boy to pretend.

JEFF. Poor Hannibal can't play—yet he does. I really can—but I won't. Don't you think that's funny?

MRS. SAVAGE. Not very.

FAIRY. *(Rushes in from hallway and screams.)* There's a rat in the hall—a rat as big as a mouse! Climb up on a chair quickly, Mrs. Savage. *(Miss Willie follows calmly, carrying tray with coffee service. Florence and Hannibal follow.)*

MISS WILLIE. Fairy—what am I going to do with you!

FLORENCE. You've put me right off my coffee.

MISS WILLIE. You know there's no rat in the hall.

FAIRY. But Mrs. Savage doesn't. She's bored here and I intend to make life exciting for her.

MRS. SAVAGE. Thank you, Fairy. You'll be happy to know that I just aged fifty years. That puts me well over the hundred mark.

FAIRY. Oh, then we must have a birthday party. I'll make candles.

MISS WILLIE. You'll sit down quietly and drink your coffee.

HANNIBAL. Oh, dear—I ate too much again. *(Stands upstage and begins bending over, trying to touch his toes.)*

FLORENCE. You shouldn't exercise right after a meal, Hannibal.

HANNIBAL. I know, but if I wait till I'm comfortable—my conscience won't needle me.

MRS. SAVAGE. *(Goes up to Miss Willie.)* Are you *sure* there've been no calls or messages for me today?

MISS WILLIE. Positive.

MRS. SAVAGE. Well—is it possible to send to the village and get tonight's— *(Whispers.)* newspaper?

MISS WILLIE. Well, if you'll serve the coffee, I'll ask Doctor Emmett.

MRS. SAVAGE. Gladly.

MISS WILLIE. *(Takes cup already poured over to Jeff, seated on piano stool.)* Here you are, Bingo.

JEFF. Florence hasn't been served.

FLORENCE. Don't stand on manners, Jeff—Miss Willie knows just how you like your coffee. I'll get my own.

JEFF. Very well. Thank you.

MISS WILLIE. You're annoyed.

JEFF. You single me out for attention, Miss Willie. It's not fair and it makes me uncomfortable.

MISS WILLIE. Jeff—I'm so tired tonight—I didn't remember. You'll have to forgive me.

JEFF. *(Smiles.)* Of course. I forget, too. *(Miss Willie goes out L. Mrs. Savage takes over coffee service. Fairy wanders to mirror and looks at herself.)*

FAIRY. Mirror, mirror on the wall—who is the best dressed of them all? *(Listens attentively.)* Fairy who?

MRS. SAVAGE. Cream in your coffee, Fairy?

FAIRY. Please. Do you think this dress does anything for me? I made it myself.

MRS. SAVAGE. It's sheer delight, Fairy. Sugar?

FAIRY. Five. *(Crosses to take cup.)* There wasn't time to finish it. I put it together with pins.

MRS. SAVAGE. Hannibal?

HANNIBAL. No, thank you. *(Bends over again.)*

MRS. SAVAGE. Would you like to know a trick to make that exercise enjoyable, Hannibal?

HANNIBAL. An enjoyable way of losing weight has yet to be invented.

MRS. SAVAGE. Well—I know of an improvement. *(Opens a drawer in table.)* All you need is a deck of cards.

FAIRY. I went to a fortune teller when I was fourteen. Everything he told me turned out wrong. I never believed in cards after that.

FLORENCE. Fairy—Fairy—Fairy!

MRS. SAVAGE. *(Takes deck of cards, hands them to Hannibal.)* Throw them up in the air.

HANNIBAL. *(Backs away.)* Why?

MRS. SAVAGE. To lose weight. *(Tosses deck into the air. Cards fall scattered on floor.)* Now all you have to do is lean over and pick them up again. One by one.

FAIRY. Oh, I like that—it's tidy.

MRS. SAVAGE. I learned it in a beauty course.

HANNIBAL. Thank you, Mrs. Savage. (*As he picks up cards.*) It's a great improvement.

FAIRY. Wouldn't it be easier to pick them up sideways?

HANNIBAL. Much. Man was made all wrong. His stomach should be in back. When he bends—it's in the way. When he kneels, his legs buckle out instead of folding neatly behind him. And why should his nose be in front? It only gets in the way when he kisses.

FAIRY. Oh, you're so right!

HANNIBAL. I guess God was in a hurry. (*Door L. opens and Dr. Emmett enters.*)

DR. EMMETT. Well, Hannibal—what are we doing now?

HANNIBAL. We're losing weight.

DR. EMMETT. Well, would you postpone it for a little while? (*Turns to others.*) Would you all go upstairs to the study for a few moments? I want to talk to Mrs. Savage. Florence, would you take the coffee up with you?

FLORENCE. (*Starts for door with tray.*) Oh, I do hate having coffee upstairs—it's so middle-class. (*Looks around.*) Where is John Thomas?

JEFF. I think you left him up on the phonograph, Florence.

FLORENCE. Oh, yes—he adores the classics.

FAIRY. Upstairs—downstairs—till I think I'll scream. May I stay, Doctor Emmett?

DR. EMMETT. No, you may not. (*All leave. Dr. Emmett turns to Mrs. Savage.*) Miss Willie tells me you seem anxious to see tonight's papers. Why?

MRS. SAVAGE. Habit.

DR. EMMETT. Here they are. (*Hands her a paper. She takes it to sofa.*) It will undoubtedly please you to know that you've caused considerable trouble again.

MRS. SAVAGE. Have I? (*Opening paper.*) Oh—Titus—on the front page. (*Reads.*) "Senator trapped in White House hothouse."

DR. EMMETT. I've just been talking to him. He's exceedingly angry.

MRS. SAVAGE. Imagine—pulling up all those petunias! What will everyone think?

DR. EMMETT. As a result of this, your position here has deteriorated considerably.

MRS. SAVAGE. And my disposition has blossomed enormously. Anything about Samuel?

DR. EMMETT. Oh, yes. (*Hands her a second paper.*) Here's the Boston *Post.*

MRS. SAVAGE. (*Reads it with delight.*) Dear, oh dear! Poor Samuel. All those bricks right on top of him. (*Reads.*) "Chimney collapses on Boston jurist." (*Looks up cheerfully.*) Well, for some people—it takes a ton of bricks, you know.

DR. EMMETT. How could they possibly have believed you?

MRS. SAVAGE. They should be committed, shouldn't they? (*Turns the pages.*) Nothing about Lily Belle?

DR. EMMETT. (*Handing her a third paper.*) Your batting average for mischief is a hundred per cent, Mrs. Savage.

MRS. SAVAGE. (*Takes paper.*) What a horrible picture of Lily Belle! This would frighten even Fairy.

DR. EMMETT. According to this, she resisted arrest.

MRS. SAVAGE. So I see. "Female Vandal Invades Museum. Berserk Heiress Bites Police." (*Looks up.*) Now they really are fools, aren't they, Doctor?

DR. EMMETT. What do you hope to gain, Mrs. Savage?

MRS. SAVAGE. Better terms.

DR. EMMETT. For your freedom?

MRS. SAVAGE. For my husband's Memorial Fund.

DR. EMMETT. Your children believe that money can be put to better use.

MRS. SAVAGE. Of course—their own. Lily Belle settled over a million dollars on her six husbands. Samuel and Titus spent as much to secure jobs to which they had no right. Is that better use?

DR. EMMETT. They consider your Memorial Fund most unorthodox, Mrs. Savage.

MRS. SAVAGE. That's absurd. There are plenty of charities for foolish people in desperate need, and none for people with a desperate need to be foolish.

DR. EMMETT. What brought you to that conclusion?

MRS. SAVAGE. My own life. No matter what we have, we never forget the foolish things we never got. I'm sure that if Hannibal had been given a violin when he wanted one, he wouldn't need one now.

DR. EMMETT. That's quite possible.

MRS. SAVAGE. I want my husband to be remembered with warmth and gratitude for a few foolish dreams that came true. I will not give up my Memorial to him.

DR. EMMETT. I want to discuss this with you further—but at the moment you have visitors waiting. *(Goes to door.)* You may come in now, Senator. *(Stands aside to let Titus, Lily Belle, and Samuel enter. Samuel's arm is in a sling.)* I'll be just outside—if you want me. *(Steps out, leaving them alone. No one speaks for a moment.)*

MRS. SAVAGE. My headache's gone.

LILY BELLE. How dare you make a fool of me! How dare you!

SAMUEL. You tried to kill me. You knew that old chimney would fall if I started pulling bricks out—didn't you?

MRS. SAVAGE. We're really not a very bright family, are we?

TITUS. Oh, you must be proud indeed to see the name of Savage held up to ridicule again!

MRS. SAVAGE. Did you dig, Titus?

TITUS. *Eight* F.B.I. men jumped me—pushed my face in the dirt. Thought I was planting a bomb.

LILY BELLE. Why didn't you tell the papers the truth? I did. *(Picks up one of the papers and reads.)* "Sleep-walking." Really!

TITUS. *(Snatches papers away from her.)* You try to think of an excuse with eight men on your chest!

MRS. SAVAGE. She'd love the chance.

TITUS. *(Reading.)* "It was learned today that the Senator's mother, Mrs. Ethel P. Savage, the actress, was recently committed for irresponsible actions. Democratic leaders were quick to point out that this might explain the career of strange behavior in Congress by the Senator." *(Hurls paper to the floor.)* Do you realize what this does to me politically?

MRS. SAVAGE. Makes you a *mort canard*. "Dead duck"—French—remember?

TITUS. I'll never survive it—never.

LILY BELLE. They treated *me* like a common criminal! I was finger-printed!

MRS. SAVAGE. Oh, I meant to ask you, Lily Belle—what is in a stuffed porpoise?

TITUS. Do you know what the papers call us now?

SAMUEL. The Mad Savages.

MRS. SAVAGE. How do you like it?

TITUS. What happened to those bonds!

MRS. SAVAGE. What happened to your dignity?

LILY BELLE. Where is my money?

MRS. SAVAGE. Where is your self-respect?

TITUS. May I ask just what you intend to do now?

MRS. SAVAGE. Are you ready to listen to my terms—or would you care to dig in Grant's Tomb?

TITUS. We are prepared to compromise.

MRS. SAVAGE. If that means you'll see things my way—then "compromise" is the right word.

TITUS. I will consider effecting your release in the custody of someone for a period of time. It would look better for us.

LILY BELLE. And I'd be willing to give her complete freedom if she'd give up acting and lead a dignified life.

MRS. SAVAGE. Freedom—as Titus can tell you—is the right to make the wrong choice.

TITUS. What would we get?

MRS. SAVAGE. That's what I like about you, Titus—no nonsense. You will each receive a reasonable yearly allowance.

SAMUEL. How reasonable?

MRS. SAVAGE. I shall be generous. But the bulk of the estate *must* be given away by my Fund.

LILY BELLE. It's completely mad.

TITUS. We might have the commitment revoked only to have you play another trick on us. Where would we be then?

MRS. SAVAGE. Where are you now?

LILY BELLE. Get it over with, Titus. *(Goes to window seat, picks up magazine.)*

TITUS. Very well. *(Turns to Samuel.)* Write a retraction, Samuel.

SAMUEL. *(Takes out fountain pen.)* I'm tired of having my decisions reversed.

MRS. SAVAGE. When I'm released, I'll keep my promise. But I warn you—don't have me followed.

LILY BELLE. Samuel—wait a minute!

TITUS. What is it?

LILY BELLE. I've found the answer…on the cover of this medical journal.

TITUS. What are you talking about!

LILY BELLE. A way to avoid your compromise. *(Folds magazine.)* But I have to see Doctor Emmett first. *(Starts for door.)*

MRS. SAVAGE. Are you going to sign that petition, Lily Belle?

LILY BELLE. Titus—don't you sign *anything* until I come back. *(Goes out quickly.)*

TITUS. Lily Belle! *(Turns to Samuel.)* What could she have read?

SAMUEL. God knows.

MRS. SAVAGE. Something to trick you. If you listen to her again, you'll end up without a cent.

SAMUEL. What'll I do?

TITUS. Finish it. Lily Belle has got us into trouble enough.

MRS. SAVAGE. And be quick. Your and Samuel's signature will be enough.

SAMUEL. *(Begins to write—and stops.)* How many "T"s in "Commitment"?

TITUS. Three.

MRS. SAVAGE. Two.

SAMUEL. *(Studies it.)* It doesn't look right.

TITUS. *(Snatches paper from him.)* I'll write it. Give me your pen.

SAMUEL. *(Hands his pen over.)* Give it back.

TITUS. *(As he writes.)* All it needs to say is the commitment was ill-advised, and request release. *(Finishes and turns to Mrs. Savage.)* Will that satisfy you?

MRS. SAVAGE. It will, when you sign it.

TITUS. Sign it, Samuel. *(Signs. Titus bends over to put signature on paper. Lily Belle returns.)*

LILY BELLE. What are you doing?

TITUS. We are signing the letter. Sign it, Lily Belle.

LILY BELLE. It isn't necessary. *(Takes paper from him and tears it up.)*

MRS. SAVAGE. You'll regret this. *(Rises.)*

TITUS. Lily Belle—you've no right to act without consulting us.

LILY BELLE. Oh, do be quiet. *(Takes magazine and hands it to Titus.)* Read that.

TITUS. Read what?

LILY BELLE. The article on Sodium Pentothal. It's— *(Dr. Emmett enters.)* Perhaps I'd better let Doctor Emmett explain. Will you tell them what Sodium Pentothal does, Doctor?

DR. EMMETT. It's generally used in cases of shock—it releases tension—removes the patients' inhibitions and makes them receptive to suggestion.

LILY BELLE. It's called the "truth drug."

DR. EMMETT. That's not quite accurate, however.

LILY BELLE. But under its influence the patient answers truthfully—isn't that so?

DR. EMMETT. If they answer at all.

LILY BELLE. *(Triumphantly, to Titus.)* Now do you understand?

MISS WILLIE. *(Enters, stands at door.)* Did you want me, Doctor?

DR. EMMETT. Yes—just a moment.

TITUS. Doctor Emmett—get some of this truth drug at once and administer it to my mother.

MRS. SAVAGE. Haven't I any rights at all, Doctor?

MISS WILLIE. Doctor Emmett—may I say something—surely you're not going to listen to these people. It's a flagrant misuse of science.

TITUS. Doctor—I order you to give my mother this drug at once.

DR. EMMETT. Mrs. Savage—if I refuse—your guardians are quite within their legal rights to remove you from my authority. I am confident they will find the means of subjecting you to the influence of Sodium Pentothal elsewhere.

MISS WILLIE. Then—let someone else be responsible, Doctor.

DR. EMMETT. *(Turns to Mrs. Savage.)* Ten million dollars hidden from use—does no one any good—least of all you. It remains an ever-present symptom of psychotic thinking. This is your opportunity to prove you are capable of making a rational decision. An intelligent mind recognizes defeat.

MRS. SAVAGE. Well—let it be known that I was not forced to my knees by science. I will tell you where the bonds are. They are— *(Sliding doors are thrown open and Florence, Hannibal, Jeffrey, and Fairy rush in.)*

FAIRY. Wait! We've come to the rescue!

FLORENCE. It's not too late.

HANNIBAL. We'll stand by you, Mrs. Savage.

FAIRY. We just happened to be listening. *(Pointing a finger.)* Shame on you—and you! And *you.*

TITUS. Doctor Emmett—*who* are these people?

MRS. SAVAGE. These are my friends.

DR. EMMETT. Weren't you asked to stay upstairs, Hannibal?

JEFF. I want to protest, Doctor.

TITUS. Who gives you the right to protest, sir? This doesn't concern you.

MRS. SAVAGE. I love you all for wanting to help me. But Doctor Emmett hasn't much choice—as you must have heard.

JEFF. What will you do, Mrs. Savage?

MRS. SAVAGE. Give them the bonds.

DR. EMMETT. I think you've made the right decision, Mrs. Savage.

TITUS. Are you going to tell us, or not?

MRS. SAVAGE. I'm going to *show* you. *(Picks up bear and looks at it fondly.)* We are going to show you. *(Takes bear's head and begins to twist it.)*

FAIRY. Oh, you'll hurt it! *(Head comes off and Mrs. Savage reaches into body and takes out bonds. All eyes are riveted on Mrs. Savage. Mrs. Paddy enters from hall and watches for a fascinated moment, unobserved.)*

MRS. SAVAGE. Here's your treasure. *(Takes packet and drops it on table. The entire group is stunned for a moment. Mrs. Paddy sees the unguarded light switch. Makes her way toward it with despatch and determination.)*

LILY BELLE. My God—she had them with her all the time! *(The three Savages make a dash for table. Before they gain their objective, Mrs. Paddy has reached light switch. The room is thrown into darkness and confusion.)*

SAMUEL. What happened to the lights!

FAIRY. Mrs. Paddy's here. Oh, Mrs. Paddy? Mrs. Paddy?

TITUS. *Where* is the light switch? *Someone* turn those lights on!

DR. EMMETT. Just a moment—I'll turn them back on.

LILY BELLE. For God's sake, Titus! Don't move. Someone might kill you.

SAMUEL. Titus—strike a match.

TITUS. I haven't got a match!

SAMUEL. Who is this?

LILY BELLE. It's me. Let go of me!

TITUS. Turn on those lights! Do you hear me! *(Lights go on. Dr. Emmett stands by switch. Hannibal is nearest the table. Lily Belle has disappeared. So has Mrs. Paddy.)* Who turned those lights off?

DR. EMMETT. *(Looking into hall.)* One of our patients. *(Calls down the hall.)* Oh, Mrs. Paddy!

SAMUEL. *(Looks around puzzled.)* Where's Lily Belle?

TITUS. She's disappeared!

FAIRY. *(Looks behind sofa.)* My gracious—what are you doing down there? *(Lily Belle rises from floor. Her hat is tilted over one eye.)*

LILY BELLE. *Somebody* pushed me.

HANNIBAL. It wasn't me. I wasn't near enough.

TITUS. *(White and drained—points a dramatic finger at table.)* They're gone! The bonds are gone! *(They race to table and search for bonds frantically.)*

LILY BELLE. Gone!

TITUS. *(Turns to Mrs. Savage.)* *What* did you do with them?

MRS. SAVAGE. I put them on the table. You saw me do it yourself.

TITUS. Then where are they?

HANNIBAL. Excuse me, Senator. I'd say that Mrs. Paddy has them. It seems obvious to me she turned off the lights, took the bonds, and ran.

DR. EMMETT. Miss Willie—get Mrs. Paddy. Notify all guards to stop her before she destroys those bonds. *(Miss Willie rushes out.)*

LILY BELLE. *(Sinks into chair C.)* I can't bear it! I simply can't bear it. I'm going to pieces.

HANNIBAL. *(Throws cards into the air above her.)* This will calm you. Would you like to try it? *(He circles her, picking them up.)*

MRS. SAVAGE. *(Rising gleefully.)* Darling Mrs. Paddy! Come on, girls. *(To Fairy and Florence.)* Let's go for a walk. *(She begins pacing the edge of the carpet, followed by Florence and Fairy. Samuel begins patting Lily Belle's wrist.)*

TITUS. Why— *(Choking.)* this is simply a *madhouse*!

CURTAIN

ACT III

SCENE: *The same.*

TIME: *A few minutes later.*

AT RISE: *The entire group sit waiting—with the exception of Titus, who paces the floor. Glances at his watch with annoyance. Lily Belle beats a nervous tattoo on arm of her chair. House phone rings. Dr. Emmett picks up receiver. All listen intently.*

DR. EMMETT. Yes, Miss Wilhelmina. Good. *(Pauses.)* Good. *(Pauses again.)* Good. *(Hangs up.)*

TITUS. *(Relieved.)* Well?

DR. EMMETT. All the wards have been locked off. The staff is alerted and Miss Willie is searching the basement now.

TITUS. But did she find that woman?

DR. EMMETT. Not yet.

TITUS. Then what in Heaven's name was the good-good-good about!

DR. EMMETT. We're taking every possible precaution, Senator.

TITUS. That maniac has ten million dollars' worth of negotiable bonds. If they're not found—they can't be replaced.

LILY BELLE. What will she do with them, Doctor?

FAIRY. Oh, she'll probably eat them.

DR. EMMETT. I don't know. But we're sure to recover them. It may take a little time.

MRS. SAVAGE. Years, probably.

LILY BELLE. *(Sits down and moans.)* They were right in front of us. Within our grasp. *(Turns on Titus in futile anger.)* Why didn't you stop her?

TITUS. How did I know the lights were going out!

MRS. SAVAGE. It's quite possible Mrs. Paddy didn't take them at all.

LILY BELLE. Of course she did. No one else *could* have taken them!

MRS. SAVAGE. *You* could have.

TITUS. Lily Belle was ten feet away from the table.

MRS. SAVAGE. But she's mighty quick when it comes to money. Personally, I think she took them and stuck them down her front. Heaven knows there's room. Why don't you search her?

SAMUEL. *(Suspiciously.)* You—you didn't take them, did you, Lily Belle?

LILY BELLE. Can't you see she's trying to make us suspect each other?

TITUS. Well—someone else *could* have taken them. *(Looks around suspiciously and suddenly points to Hannibal.)* He was nearest the table when the lights went out.

LILY BELLE. He was right beside it.

TITUS. Well—what have you got to say?

HANNIBAL. *(Backs away under Titus' accusation.)* I didn't take them. I don't like bonds. *(Throws his cards nervously in the air.)*

FAIRY. *(Shrieks and points to a card on the floor.)* The Queen of Spades! Someone is going to die!

LILY BELLE. Doctor Emmett—must we have these people here?

TITUS. Get them out of here. *(Then as quickly changes his mind.)* No—no! Don't let anyone out of our sight until he's searched.

MRS. SAVAGE. Everybody off with his clothes!

FAIRY. My glasses, too?

DR. EMMETT. Fairy—just a moment. Mrs. Savage—please don't make this any more difficult than you already have.

LILY BELLE. *(Halts in front of Hannibal.)* And for heaven's sake— do something about this man's tossing cards around. My nerves are on edge.

DR. EMMETT. Hannibal. Don't. *(Hannibal sits down meekly.)*

FAIRY.   Don't-do-this-don't-do-that-don't-do-this-don't-do-that. *(Rises to face Lily Belle.)* I understand that you have a lovely tiara. Do you sleep in it?

LILY BELLE. Oh, sit down, you unattractive creature! I've had quite enough.

FAIRY. *(Stares at her a moment.)* I don't like you.

DR. EMMETT. Fairy—will you please sit down and be quiet while we wait.

FAIRY. Very well. *(Sits down beside Hannibal and Jeff, and hiccups.)*

FLORENCE. *(Pained.)* Fairy!

FAIRY. Excuse me. I'm upset. *(Puts hand over her mouth. And with Jeff covering his face and ears, and Hannibal shading his eyes, they unintentionally form a quiet picture of "Hear no evil, see no evil, speak no evil." Everyone is quiet for a moment. Then behind them the doors slip open and Mrs. Paddy backs slowly into the room, peering down hall from which she eludes her hunters. Closes sliding doors carefully and holds them together. Dr. Emmett walks quietly up behind her.)*

DR. EMMETT. Well, Mrs. Paddy—you have the entire staff searching for you. *(Mrs. Paddy whirls around and faces the roomful of people rather sheepishly. Tries to dart out again.)*

TITUS. Stop her—don't let her get away!

DR. EMMETT. *(Steps in front of her.)* I think you'd better join us, Mrs. Paddy. We'd like to talk to you. *(Points to a chair c. and escorts Mrs. Paddy to it. With Olympian dignity, she seats herself, ignoring visitors and patients alike.)*

TITUS. Now, we'll find out where those bonds are. *(Mrs. Paddy, with an air of disdain, brushes imaginary crumbs off her ample bosom. Titus strides over to Mrs. Paddy.)* Madam—hand over those bonds!

DR. EMMETT. You'd better let me question her, Senator. She won't talk to you.

TITUS. Oh, yes, she will.

MRS. SAVAGE. Oh, no, she won't.

TITUS. We'll just see about this. *(Roars at Mrs. Paddy, who winces at the blast.)* Well, madam—what have you to say for yourself!

MRS. PADDY. *(Turns and glares up at Titus.)* I hate everything in the world, but most of all I hate revolving doors, cuspidors, fights, fuzz, fleas, bumblebees, prickly heat, bats, gnats, pills, pots, pans, butts, bladders, worms, germs, pachyderms, and politicians!

TITUS. *(Stopped—for the moment.)* What does she mean?

MRS. SAVAGE. Weren't you listening?

FAIRY. *(Hiccups.)* Excuse me, please.

FLORENCE. Fairy!

TITUS. Madam, did you hear what I asked you?

DR. EMMETT. *(Steps in front of Titus.)* There's no need to shout at Mrs. Paddy, Senator. She hears you well enough. But she's not going to answer you. She hasn't answered a question in twenty years.

TITUS. *(Turns on Mrs. Paddy again.)* Don't try any tricks on me, madam!

MRS. SAVAGE. Don't make her mad, Titus—she carries a knife. *(Titus takes a quick step back.)*

DR. EMMETT. Please—Mrs. Savage. *(Turns to Titus.)* Mrs. Paddy doesn't carry a knife. She's hostile but quite harmless. Now, will you be kind enough to yield the floor to me, Senator?

TITUS. Very well—but I want to hear her talk.

MRS. SAVAGE. So do we all.

DR. EMMETT. *(Kneels down beside Mrs. Paddy.)* Mrs. Paddy— this is quite important. Now I want you to nod Yes or No to the questions I ask you. *(Mrs. Paddy looks at him vacantly.)* Now. Did you take some bonds from the table a few minutes ago? *(Mrs. Paddy waits—nods a vigorous "Yes" followed by a vigorous "No.")*

MRS. SAVAGE. She did and she didn't.

FAIRY. Oh, this is exciting. I wish we could open a door and have a body fall out.

DR. EMMETT. Mrs. Paddy—look at me. *(She gives him her rapt attention.)* Do you remember turning the lights out? *(Mrs. Paddy nods "No.")* Yes, you do. And do you remember a little bundle of papers on the table? *(Mrs. Paddy stares at top of his head.)* Try to remember— think. *(Mrs. Paddy leans forward and dutifully assumes the pose of the Rodin Thinker. While they watch for some manifestation of understanding, Miss Willie comes in from hall, carrying a shoe-box.)*

MISS WILLIE. Doctor Emmett—I found them! *(Mrs. Paddy leaps to her feet and rushes for box.)*

TITUS. *(Beside her in one stride.)* No, you don't! Hand them over to me!

MISS WILLIE. But, Senator—

TITUS. I'll take charge of these. *(Takes box from her hand and jerks top off. The contents pour on the floor.)*

FAIRY. Oh, look—radio tubes!

TITUS. You said you'd found the bonds!

MISS WILLIE. I said nothing of the sort. *(Mrs. Paddy gets down on her knees to collect her own treasure.)*

FAIRY. This restores my faith in witchcraft.

DR. EMMETT. Where did you find them, Miss Willie?

MISS WILLIE. In the basement—in the hot-air duct leading to Fairy's room.

FAIRY. I told you I was cold all winter and you wouldn't believe me!

TITUS. I hold you completely responsible for this fiasco, Doctor.

DR. EMMETT. Just what would you suggest that I do, Senator?

TITUS. Search that woman—she may have them hidden on her person! *(Mrs. Paddy immediately abandons tubes, seats herself and winds her legs around legs of chair and grips arms.)*

DR. EMMETT. I'm afraid this is going to present a problem.

TITUS. Then search everyone else while we concentrate on making her talk.

DR. EMMETT. Very well. *(Turns to Miss Willie.)* Will you take Mrs. Savage to her room and search her, please?

FAIRY. No—no—no. Take me. I'm the youngest and undress quickest. *(Turns to Mrs. Savage.)* Or do you want to draw straws?

MRS. SAVAGE. You first, Fairy. I don't want to miss anything.

FAIRY. Thank you.

MISS WILLIE. Would you like to come with me, Fairy?

FAIRY. Oh, yes. *(She links her arm in Miss Willie's and they start for door.)* Do you know I was once asked to play Lady Godiva for the Elks' Pageant. But I didn't.—My mother was afraid of so many Elks. *(Goes out with Miss Willie.)*

DR. EMMETT. Mrs. Paddy—wouldn't you like to save us a lot of trouble? *(She looks at him blankly.)*

LILY BELLE. Haven't you some kind of threat you resort to here?

DR. EMMETT. I don't threaten my patients. Mrs. Paddy—look at me.

LILY BELLE. The truth drug!

TITUS. Of course! Use the truth drug on her. Then we can make her talk.

DR. EMMETT. I'm afraid it's out of the question. I'd have to have her guardian's consent.

TITUS. Very well—we'll get it. Who is her guardian?

DR. EMMETT. Her husband.

TITUS. *(Going to phone.)* We'll get him on the phone. Where is he?

DR. EMMETT. Japan. *(Titus stops.)*

TITUS. Well, in his absence—haven't you the authority to act?

DR. EMMETT. We've no proof that she took them yet.

MRS. SAVAGE. I still think Lily Belle's your girl.

LILY BELLE. *Will* you stop saying that!

JEFF. Doctor Emmett…

DR. EMMETT. Yes, Jeff?

JEFF. Since Mrs. Savage can't have her bonds anyhow, I think I can help you.

DR. EMMETT. Yes?

JEFF. Mrs. Paddy didn't take them.

DR. EMMETT. How do you know?

JEFF. Because I took them.

TITUS. He's the thief! I knew we were being tricked. *(Strides over to Jeff.)* Hand them over, young man.

JEFF. I—I can't.

DR. EMMETT. Did you take them, Jeffrey?

JEFF. Yes, sir.

DR. EMMETT. Then what did you do with them? *(Before Jeff answers, Miss Willie enters.)*

MISS WILLIE. I've searched Fairy, Doctor. She doesn't have them.

TITUS. *(Ignores Miss Willie, to Jeff.)* Speak up!

JEFF. I—I threw them out the window.

LILY BELLE. *(Rushes to window, followed by Samuel.)* Go outside, quickly, Titus—we'll watch from the window.

FLORENCE. *(Rises in their path.)* Stop! *(Points to board.)* Parcheesi—the royal game of India!

DR. EMMETT. But, Jeff—you couldn't have thrown them out the window—the window is closed.

JEFF. Oh.

SAMUEL. It's stuck.

TITUS. *(Grabs Jeff by his lapels.)* What do you mean by misleading us! *(Miss Willie charges down on Titus.)*

MISS WILLIE. Let go of him—you stupid ox!

TITUS. *(Cowed by her sudden fury.)* He—he said he took the bonds!

MISS WILLIE. Well, he didn't. I happen to know he didn't.

TITUS. And just how do you happen to know that?

MISS WILLIE. That's none of your business.

DR. EMMETT. How do you know, Miss Willie?

MISS WILLIE. *(Angrily.)* Because I had my arms around Jeff when the lights went out. I wanted to protect him from being hurt during the confusion.

DR. EMMETT. Thank you, Miss Willie.

JEFF. But she didn't. That's not true. I took them. No one else. *(They turn to the doors as they are flung open and Fairy makes a dramatic entrance.)*

FAIRY. Doctor Emmett! Miss Willie! Something awful is happening. There's a fire upstairs. With flames— *(Measures as high as she can reach.)* this high!

FLORENCE. Fairy—you mustn't—we've company.

FAIRY. Well, they were— *(She amends the distance.)* this high, at least.

DR. EMMETT. Fairy—come in and sit there quietly, please.

FAIRY. But there's a fire. Please believe me—there's a fire upstairs.

DR. EMMETT. Where?

FAIRY. *(Hesitates.)* In the bathtub.

DR. EMMETT. *(Firmly.)* Fairy—sit down.

FAIRY. *(As she goes to piano stool.)* I can't—I'm full of pins.

DR. EMMETT. *(Turns to Jeff.)* Jeff—if you did take the bonds—
where did you put them?

MISS WILLIE. I told you—he couldn't have taken them.

FLORENCE. Of course he couldn't. If anyone should know that—
I should.

TITUS. Now, I suppose *you* took them?

FLORENCE. I confess everything.

FAIRY. *(Plaintively.)* There's a fire upstairs.

LILY BELLE. There's a conspiracy down here!

DR. EMMETT. Where are they, Florence?

FLORENCE. I won't tell you.

TITUS. These people are trying to deceive us.

FLORENCE. I have committed this theft with full knowledge of
the stigma involved.

FAIRY. Something's burning upstairs.

SAMUEL. Better search her.

FLORENCE. Greedy little man.

DR. EMMETT. *(Turns to Miss Willie.)* Will you take Florence to
her room and search her carefully?

MISS WILLIE. Come along, Florence.

FLORENCE. *(To Mrs. Savage.)* I'll never tell, Mrs. Savage—even if
they put me in solitary confinement and cut off all my hair. *(Goes out.)*

HANNIBAL. It's a waste of time to search dear Florence.

TITUS. Now I suppose *you* took them?

HANNIBAL. No—but I know who did.

FAIRY. I know a fire when I see one.

DR. EMMETT. Who did, Hannibal?

HANNIBAL. It wasn't Mrs. Paddy.

TITUS. Who was it!

HANNIBAL. It wasn't Florence, either.

TITUS. I don't want to know who it *wasn't*—I want to know who was it!

MRS. SAVAGE. Is that good grammar?

HANNIBAL. If you ask a Mohammedan what God is, he'll name all the things He isn't—it's easier than telling what He is.

MRS. SAVAGE. And one of the things He isn't is—He isn't on your side.

DR. EMMETT. Hannibal—if you know who took the bonds—will you tell us?

HANNIBAL. I'm not sure who took them, but I know it was a woman, and I know it wasn't Mrs. Paddy.

FAIRY. Oh, fiddle—let the house burn!

DR. EMMETT. How do you know?

HANNIBAL. A woman pushed me out of the way to get them.

TITUS. How do you know it was a woman?

MRS. SAVAGE. Really, Titus!

DR. EMMETT. How do you know it was not Mrs. Paddy?

HANNIBAL. She doesn't use perfume.

MRS. SAVAGE. Lily Belle bathes in it.

LILY BELLE. I was nowhere near the table.

SAMUEL. Could you identify the scent?

HANNIBAL. I think so.

MRS. SAVAGE. Well, I use gardenia—what do you use, Fairy?

FAIRY. No name—I make my own.

MRS. SAVAGE. Hannibal—smell Lily Belle.

LILY BELLE. Titus—I won't tolerate this—they're making fools of us for their own amusement.

MRS. SAVAGE. *(As Hannibal sniffs toward Lily Belle.)* Smell anything, Hannibal?

HANNIBAL. Yes!

MRS. SAVAGE. What?

HANNIBAL. *(Frowns.)* Smoke.

FAIRY. High time.

TITUS. I must be losing my mind—I smell smoke, too! *(Doors open and Miss Willie comes in, holding a basin full of smoldering papers.)*

MISS WILLIE. Doctor Emmett. I found a fire in Mrs. Paddy's bathtub.

FAIRY. I *don't* think I'll speak to anyone!

DR. EMMETT. In the *bathtub*?

MISS WILLIE. I'm afraid it's the bonds. *(Takes basin down C.)* Or what's left of them.

LILY BELLE. Oh, no! *(Sinks into a chair.)* No—no—no—no—no!

TITUS. Let me see! *(Examines ashes.)* Why, there's no way of telling what these are.

DR. EMMETT. Mrs. Paddy—did you take those bonds to your room and set fire to them? *(Mrs. Paddy looks up at him blankly, nods "Yes" and "No," and sits down.)*

MISS WILLIE. Senator here's a part of something that didn't burn— can you tell what it is?

TITUS. *(Examines it, then wipes his brow.)* It's the burnt end of a half-million-dollar bond.

DR. EMMETT. Are you sure? *(Takes it over to Mrs. Savage.)* Mrs. Savage, can you identify this?

MRS. SAVAGE. Well, the treasure hunt is over. It's all that's left of ten million dollars.

FAIRY. I should have told a lie—then someone would have believed me.

DR. EMMETT. Yes, I'm sorry, Fairy. I should have believed you anyhow. There must be some way of having them replaced, Senator?

TITUS. Well, there isn't.

LILY BELLE. They can't be gone—they just can't.

TITUS. *(Crosses to Mrs. Paddy.)* You miserable, useless creature— do you know what you've cost us!

MRS. SAVAGE. *(Puts her arms about Mrs. Paddy.)* Oh—let her alone! *(Mrs. Paddy begins to cry.)* Never mind, Mrs. Paddy—

DR. EMMETT. I've stood for as much bullying of my patients as I intend to—now will you be so kind as to leave—at once?

LILY BELLE. What about the burnt piece—isn't it worth anything?

TITUS. Nothing. *(Turns to Dr. Emmett.)* I hold you personally responsible.

LILY BELLE. I can't be poor—I don't know how!

TITUS. It's all right, Lily Belle—we'll survive. We always have. I am still Senator.

MRS. SAVAGE. Lily Belle—I never intended it to end like this, believe me.

LILY BELLE. Take me home, Titus—please. *(Leaning on Titus, she goes to door held open by Miss Willie.)*

MRS. SAVAGE. Titus—

TITUS. *(Stops.)* Yes?

MRS. SAVAGE. What happens to me?

TITUS. You have nothing to worry about. We would never allow you to be sent to a public institution. *(Follows Lily Belle out.)*

SAMUEL. *(Proudly.)* We are Savages!

FAIRY. Goodbye. We say goodbye to people we don't want to see again. *(Samuel goes out, and door closes behind them. Mrs. Paddy begins to cry.)*

MRS. SAVAGE. Don't cry, Mrs. Paddy. I'm sure you hate tears, too.

FAIRY. Maybe she thinks her tub is cracked?

DR. EMMETT. Did you think you could change them, Mrs. Savage?

MRS. SAVAGE. No one changes people—one makes changes people learn to accept. I had hoped to make them look like fools so they might look with understanding on the fools of good heart.

DR. EMMETT. And who are the fools of good heart, Mrs. Savage?

MRS. SAVAGE. I'd say—those who gamble on people, and invest in kindness—those who doubt that position means privilege, or that manners mean morals. And, of course, the rebels with no fear of failure.

DR. EMMETT. That makes very good sense.

MRS. SAVAGE. And justifies my being here?

DR. EMMETT. Would you like to leave?

MRS. SAVAGE. They would never let me go.

DR. EMMETT. They have nothing to say about it. No patient's commitment is final until I have made my decision. And I find no valid reason for your remaining.

MRS. SAVAGE. Does that mean—I am free?

DR. EMMETT. *(Hesitates.)* Well, I could release you on my own authority at once, but— *(Starts for door L.)* Let me get the State Medical Inspector on the telephone. Then I'll let you know definitely. *(Exits.)*

MISS WILLIE. *(Crosses to hall door.)* I think I'll pack your things— just in case. We can always unpack again. *(Goes out. Guests all turn to Mrs. Savage.)*

FAIRY. You hate us.

MRS. SAVAGE. Why do you say that, Fairy?

FAIRY. You want to leave us.

MRS. SAVAGE. Oh, Fairy—I must.

JEFF. Is someone waiting for you?

MRS. SAVAGE. No.

FLORENCE. Does someone need you?

MRS. SAVAGE. No.

FAIRY. But you can't leave! I haven't had time to get you a going-away present. Maybe I could find a suitable present anyhow—if you won't be fussy. I'll go look. *(Starts out.)*

FLORENCE. I'd like to see what I can find for you, too, Mrs. Savage. Will you wait?

FAIRY. Oh, fun!—Come on, everybody—let's see what we can find.

JEFF. I have something. I just remembered.

FAIRY. Don't leave before we get back now—or you won't get anything.

FLORENCE. I'll try to find something useless. I do abhor practical gifts. *(All leave except Hannibal.)*

HANNIBAL. There's nothing in my room you'd want, Mrs. Savage.

But I have something on me that I prize. My class ring. Inside it says, "Let there be Light." Something Mrs. Paddy would hate.

MRS. SAVAGE. No—Hannibal, I couldn't take the ring off your finger.

HANNIBAL. But I insist. It has no value as gold goes, but as blood goes, it's a statistical treasure. My heart has pumped my blood through this ring every two minutes for ten years. That adds up roughly to about a hundred thousand gallons of blood.

MRS. SAVAGE. It's *too* much, Hannibal.

HANNIBAL. *(Struggling.)* Not at all. *(Looks up unhappily.)* But I don't seem able to get it off.

MRS. SAVAGE. Keep it, Hannibal. I deeply appreciate the offer, the sentiment and the statistics.

HANNIBAL. *(Looks at his chubby finger.)* My finger has got too fat on each side of the ring.

MRS. SAVAGE. Never mind, Hannibal. You've had it so long, it has become a part of you.

FAIRY. *(Reenters and runs down to Mrs. Savage.)* Oh! I'm all out of breath! Feel my heart! *(Takes Mrs. Savage's hand and holds it over her heart.)*

MRS. SAVAGE. Why, Fairy, dear!

FAIRY. But I found something. *(Hands Mrs. Savage a hastily wrapped package.)* I hope you didn't expect much because then you won't be disappointed.

MRS. SAVAGE. I won't be disappointed.

FAIRY. *(As Mrs. Savage unwraps present.)* I couldn't find anything to wrap it in except Kleenex. *(Turns to Hannibal.)* You can feel my heart, too, Hannibal.

HANNIBAL. *(Covers her heart with his palm.)* Thank you. About 104 beats to the minute, I'd say.

MRS. SAVAGE. *(Looks down at her present.)* How very nice!

HANNIBAL. What is it?

MRS. SAVAGE. A handkerchief.

FAIRY. Oh, no! It's a napkin. So many places serve paper napkins. But they blot or smear.

MRS. SAVAGE. Bless you, Fairy, I'll take it with me whenever I'm invited out.

FAIRY. It says "The Cloisters" on it. Wasn't that lucky?

FLORENCE. *(Comes in with Jeffrey.)* Oh, Fairy found something first. What did she give you?

MRS. SAVAGE. A hand-picked napkin.

FLORENCE. Then it fits in perfectly with my present. *(Hands Mrs. Savage her gift.)* It's practical, after all. I hope you don't mind.

MRS. SAVAGE. Florence—you *shouldn't* have!

FAIRY. What is it?

HANNIBAL. A salt shaker.

MRS. SAVAGE. And full of salt, too.

FLORENCE. It's engraved. It says "The Cloisters" on it.

MRS. SAVAGE. You've gone to too much trouble.

FLORENCE. Oh—it was nothing.

FAIRY. Is it sterling?

FLORENCE. *(Turns to Fairy—patiently.)* Fairy, dear—I wouldn't dream of giving Mrs. Savage anything that wasn't sterling.

FAIRY. Oh—it's dented.

FLORENCE. Really, Fairy! Dents give an antique character.

MRS. SAVAGE. Indeed they do!

FAIRY. Well, I'm not going to say goodbye. I can't stand good-byes—I don't recognize them. *(Goes to door.)*

FLORENCE. Oh—you didn't expect us to say goodbye—did you?

MRS. SAVAGE. I didn't even expect a salt shaker.

FAIRY. Well…

FLORENCE. *(Takes Mrs. Savage's hand.)* How do you do, Mrs. Savage—we have so looked forward to meeting you.

FAIRY. We're glad you're here at last. Make yourself at home. *(Florence starts to follow Fairy to door, and stops.)*

FLORENCE. Oh—I almost forgot. John Thomas asked me to give you something from him. *(Comes back and kisses Mrs. Savage on the cheek.)* He was afraid you'd catch his measles if he delivered it himself. *(Starts out again.)* Come, Fairy—let's pretend it's Garden Hour. *(Goes out.)*

FAIRY. Excuse us, please—we have to dig weeds. *(Smiles.)* Take an umbrella—it's raining. *(Goes out.)*

HANNIBAL. Well, Jeffrey—what did you bring?

JEFF. Just a book. But I hope you enjoy it.

HANNIBAL. What is it, Mrs. Savage?

MRS. SAVAGE. *(Takes book, reads title.)* The Life Span of the Ape. *(Looks up.)* Do you know I've never read it!

JEFF. I was lucky, wasn't I?

MRS. SAVAGE. I'm going to read it tonight. *(Mrs. Paddy comes running in with something clenched in her fist.)*

HANNIBAL. We thought you'd forgotten us, Mrs. Paddy.

JEFF. What did you get, Mrs. Paddy? *(Mrs. Paddy pushes her fist out. Mrs. Savage uneasily allows her to unfold something in her palm.)*

MRS. SAVAGE. *(Opens palm and looks up, relieved.)* Now, how did you know this was just what I needed? *(Mrs. Paddy beams.)*

JEFF. May I see it?

MRS. SAVAGE. A genuine mother-of-pearl button. I'll sew it on at once. *(Holds it to her throat. Mrs. Paddy nods a furious denial. Goes over, picks up Mrs. Savage's bear and indicates its missing eye.)*

JEFF. I think it's intended to make an eye for the bear.

MRS. SAVAGE. Well, bless your angry heart—why, of course. *(Goes over to Mrs. Paddy and hugs her.)* We both thank you. He's hated having only one eye.

MRS. PADDY. I hate everything in the world… *(Stops and begins again.)* I hate everything in the world…but… *(Then finishes with the words tumbling out.)* I hate everything in the world but you, and I love you and I wish you wouldn't leave us. *(Looks up at Mrs. Savage and flees from the room.)*

MRS. SAVAGE. *(Watches after her a moment, then turns to the two men.)* Why—she said she loved me!

HANNIBAL. Well?

MRS. SAVAGE. Aren't you amazed?

JEFF. Why? We knew it all along.

MRS. SAVAGE. Yes, but she *spoke*!

JEFF. She had to—to say it.

HANNIBAL. Well, Jeff—shall we see what the girls are up to? It's a lovely night and everybody's polite. *(Goes to door and stops. Turns and speaks to Mrs. Savage.)* Watch out—don't break your neck. *(Goes out.)*

JEFF. *(Goes to door and stops.)* You have a good seat. *(Leaves quickly. Mrs. Savage stands alone a moment. Miss Willie enters.)*

MISS WILLIE. I think I have everything. Here's your eighty-five-dollar hat. I told you you'd want it again.

MRS. SAVAGE. My beautiful and foolish hat!

MISS WILLIE. You know, I think you've been wearing it backwards.

MRS. SAVAGE. *(Turns it around.)* You know—I *have*. It's good to be straightened out.

MISS WILLIE. Where did everybody go?

MRS. SAVAGE. They gave me going-away presents and then refused to say goodbye.

MISS WILLIE. I'll bet I can guess what they gave you.

MRS. SAVAGE. No, you can't. Mrs. Paddy gave me an eye with which to see myself. Florence a grain of salt to take with what I see.

MISS WILLIE. That's good. And Fairy?

MRS. SAVAGE. A memory of loveliness.

MISS WILLIE. I'm afraid to most people she wouldn't seem a lovely girl.

MRS. SAVAGE. She wears her plainness with great beauty.

MISS WILLIE. And Jeff?

MRS. SAVAGE. *(Looks at her book.)* The Book of Job.

MISS WILLIE. Nothing from Hannibal?

MRS. SAVAGE. *(Pauses.)* I'd say he gave me an appreciation of music I never had before!

MISS WILLIE. *(Laughs.)* Well, I have something to give you, too.

MRS. SAVAGE. You behave yourself.

MISS WILLIE. *(Hands her a small package.)* It isn't much.

MRS. SAVAGE. It better not be. *(Opens package.)* My bonds— *(Looks up.)*

MISS WILLIE. Except for a corner of one that I had to burn with the newspapers to make it look convincing.

MRS. SAVAGE. Oh, dear. Where did you find them?

MISS WILLIE. I didn't find them. I stole them when the lights went out.

MRS. SAVAGE. Why?

MISS WILLIE. I'm not sure.

MRS. SAVAGE. Don't tell me you're a kleptomaniac!

MISS WILLIE. *(Laughs.)* It was too quick to think. What bothers me is that after I took them, I toyed with the idea of keeping them.

MRS. SAVAGE. That's a normal impulse. What stopped you?

MISS WILLIE. What Jeff might think.

MRS. SAVAGE. You should get away from here, my dear. That kind of thinking isn't good for you.

MISS WILLIE. But you knew Jeff was my husband, didn't you?

MRS. SAVAGE. I certainly did not.

MISS WILLIE. Well, he is. I want to be here when he recovers. And do you know why I wouldn't keep any of that money? Pure selfishness. I want to do everything for him myself. Surely you understand that?

MRS. SAVAGE. The only thing I don't understand is how I could ever have felt so sorry for myself. Isn't there something about no fool like a you-know-what?

MISS WILLIE. Something. But I don't think it applies to you.

MRS. SAVAGE. *(Looks down at bonds.)* Does anyone else know about these?

MISS WILLIE. I told Doctor Emmett.

MRS. SAVAGE. Well, whether you want it or not, you're both going to hear from my Memorial Fund. *(Dr. Emmett enters.)*

DR. EMMETT. I talked to the Medical Examiner.

MRS. SAVAGE. Yes?

DR. EMMETT. The station wagon is outside ready to take you whenever you want to go. *(Turns to Miss Willie.)* Will you take Mrs. Savage's bag out to the car?

MISS WILLIE. Yes, Doctor. *(She picks up bag and goes out.)*

DR. EMMETT. I've a few papers for you to sign, Mrs. Savage—then you're free to go.

MRS. SAVAGE. Oh, I must be out of my mind, really. I don't want to go!

DR. EMMETT. You mean you'd prefer to leave tomorrow?

MRS. SAVAGE. I don't think I want to leave at all.

DR. EMMETT. Why do you want to stay?

MRS. SAVAGE. Suddenly—I'm weary. I would like to rest—I would like to be relieved of decision. I would like to be protected against uncertainty and accident. I would like to close my eyes at night and know that there are walls to guard my sleep.

DR. EMMETT. But the peace you find here is the moon reflected on a dark lake. Strike the surface and you destroy it. Is that the kind of peace you want?

MRS. SAVAGE. I want what everyone wants—to want nothing. These people have found contentment.

DR. EMMETT. How do you know?

MRS. SAVAGE. I have eyes to see.

DR. EMMETT. So has Jeffrey—but he sees only what he wants to see—an excuse for not facing the future. Does Florence see that her child was taken from her? Does Fairy see what the mirror should tell her? No. They've found refuge in an eggshell world where you don't belong. For you see yourself clearly, I'm sure.

MRS. SAVAGE. Then where *do* I belong?

DR. EMMETT. *(Rises.)* In the world you can best serve. The impulse to live your life with courage was right. Go ahead with your Memorial. *(Starts for door.)* And don't be betrayed by the illusion of contentment. *(Stops at door.)* The door is open for you. Make your peace with loneliness. *(Goes out. For a moment, Mrs. Savage stands looking about the room. Slowly she picks up bonds and ties box. Hannibal returns from hall, breathless, carrying his violin.)*

HANNIBAL. Oh—I'm glad you're still here. *(Comes over to her.)* I just thought of what I can give you.

MRS. SAVAGE. Hannibal—*not* your violin!

HANNIBAL. Oh, no, you couldn't play it! But I can give you a song you can take anywhere you go. Here is your song. *(Lifts his violin and begins to play. The same two hard notes jar the nerves again. Mrs. Savage listens with patience as he saws away. It is ugly and discordant. Mrs. Paddy comes into the room behind Mrs. Savage. She lowers her head like a charging bull, and makes for the light switch. The room is plunged into darkness. For a moment there is no sound, and then the soft muted strains of a violin are heard. The strains of Ravel's lovely "Berceuse sur le nom de Gabriel Fauré" for violin and piano are heard. Slowly, a soft center of light fades in on Mrs. Savage, who stands alone by the table L. She picks up her gifts and her bear. She turns as another soft center of light fades in R., revealing a group gathered around piano. Jeff is seated playing as he knows he can. Hannibal plays as he has always heard himself playing. Mrs. Paddy stands facing her easel. The crude canvas before her has become a finished seascape of great beauty. Seated on sofa we discover Florence. As she listens to the music, she strokes the head of a handsome little boy who clutches her hand and rests against her. As the music mounts, Fairy enters. Her hair is no longer tied in an unbecoming knot. It is free and hangs softly by her cheeks. Her gown is a dream of loveliness. It billows about her in graceful lines as she sits at Hannibal's feet. Mrs. Savage looks from one to the other, then replacing the bear upright on the table, she throws a kiss toward the guests as the picture fades. She walks slowly to door and goes out—leaving behind the lost people in their eggshell world. Only the teddy bear sitting alone in a spot of light in the surrounding darkness is seen as)*

THE CURTAIN FALLS

PROPERTY LIST

(Use this space to create props lists for your production)

SOUND EFFECTS

(Use this space to create sound effects lists for your production)

Note on Songs/Recordings, Images, or Other Production Design Elements

Be advised that Dramatists Play Service, Inc., neither holds the rights to nor grants permission to use any songs, recordings, images, or other design elements mentioned in the play. It is the responsibility of the producing theater/organization to obtain permission of the copyright owner(s) for any such use. Additional royalty fees may apply for the right to use copyrighted materials.

For any songs/recordings, images, or other design elements mentioned in the play, works in the public domain may be substituted. It is the producing theater/organization's responsibility to ensure the substituted work is indeed in the public domain. Dramatists Play Service, Inc., cannot advise as to whether or not a song/arrangement/recording, image, or other design element is in the public domain.